Eating Disorders

D0462466

Eating problems are common in children and teenagers. Yet myths about such problems abound and it can be very difficult to separate the facts from popular beliefs; unusual or disturbed eating patterns can be understandably bewildering and distressing for parents.

Whatever aspects of your child's eating behaviour is causing you concern, this book will help you understand some of the more common reasons why problems arise, and will give you advice on what you and others can do to manage the situation.

Written by experienced clinicians, *Eating Disorders: A Parents' Guide* provides positive, sensible advice on a range of eating disturbances in children and adolescents – both girls and boys – and answers many of the questions frequently asked by worried parents, including:

- Why is my child experiencing eating problems?
- What can I do to get her to talk about it?
- Where can we seek help and treatment?
- How long will it be before my child is better?

Complete with a helpful glossary, suggestions for further reading, and a list of useful addresses, *Eating Disorders: A Parents' Guide* is a reassuring and practical book that will support and encourage you and your child to obtain appropriate help and successfully deal with those worrying eating problems.

Rachel Bryant-Waugh is Consultant Clinical Psychologist and an Honorary Senior Lecturer at the University of Southampton.

Bryan Lask is Professor of Child and Adolescent Psychiatry at St George's Hospital Medical School and Medical Advisor to the Huntercombe Hospitals, UK.

Eating Disorders
A Parents' Guide

Revised Edition

Rachel Bryant-Waugh
and
Bryan Lask

Brunner-Routledge
Taylor & Francis Group

HOVE AND NEW YORK

First published in 1999
by Penguin Books Ltd.

Revised edition published in 2004
by Brunner-Routledge
27 Church Lane, Hove, East Sussex, BN3 2FA

Simultaneously published in the USA and Canada
by Brunner-Routledge
29 West 35th Street, New York, NY 10001

Brunner-Routledge is an imprint of the Taylor & Francis Group

Typeset in New Century Schoolbook by
RefineCatch Ltd, Bungay, Suffolk
Printed and bound in Great Britain by
Biddles Ltd, King's Lynn

Cover design by Terry Foley at Anú Design

British Library Cataloguing in Publication Data
A catalogue record for this book is available from the British Library

Library of Congress Cataloging-in-Publication Data

Bryant-Waugh, Rachel.
   Eating disorders: a parents' guide / Rachel Bryant-Waugh and
Bryan Lask.–Rev. ed.
      p.   cm.
   Includes bibliographical references and index.
   ISBN 1-58391-860-4 (pbk.: alk. paper)
1. Eating disorders in children–Popular works. 2. Eating disorders
in adolescence–Popular works. I. Lask, Bryan. II. Title.
RJ506.E18B79   2004
618.92'8526–dc22   2003024355

ISBN 1-58391-860-4

Dedication

This book is dedicated to the many young people with eating disorders whom we have met over the years, and to their parents. We have sympathized with their suffering, admired their courage, and rejoiced in their recovery.

When will I stop seeing food as the enemy?
When will my guilt and fear cease?
Why can't I think my thoughts clearly?
Why won't they just leave me in peace?

What does it mean to be 'normal'?
I want to have fun and be free.
When will the dark turn to daybreak?
When can I enjoy being me?

How can I kill these small demons?
Those monsters that tear up my head.
In what way can I finally defeat them?
I wish for them to be dead!

CW

Contents

About the authors

Rachel Bryant-Waugh was educated in The Netherlands and subsequently studied Human Sciences at the University of Sussex. She went on to obtain her D.Phil., also at Sussex, on the subject of childhood onset anorexia nervosa, while also working at Great Ormond Street Hospital for Children. She completed her clinical psychology training in 1988 and returned to Great Ormond Street to specialize, with Bryan Lask, in the treatment and study of eating disorders in childhood. She has published and taught widely on this subject and is currently a Consultant Clinical Psychologist and an Honorary Senior Lecturer at the University of Southampton.

Bryan Lask trained at St Bartholomew's Hospital Medical School, London, and did postgraduate training at the Maudsley Hospital and Institute of Psychiatry, and Great Ormond Street Hospital for Children. He was Consultant Psychiatrist at Great Ormond Street from 1975 to 1998 and was Director of the Eating Disorders Programme there. He is currently Professor of Child and Adolescent Psychiatry at St George's Hospital Medical School and Medical Advisor to the Huntercombe Hospitals, UK. The author of eight books and over a hundred and fifty scientific papers, he has lectured throughout the world and has been a visiting professor at a number of universities in Norway, Australia, Canada and the USA.

Dr Bryant-Waugh and Professor Lask are the co-editors of *Eating Disorders in Childhood and Early Adolescence* (Psychology Press 2000).

List of figures and tables

Foreword

When children or teenagers have unusual or disturbed eating patterns, parents are understandably bewildered, distressed and frustrated. They cannot make sense of such intense concerns about eating, often accompanied by seemingly inappropriate worries about weight and shape. This book is for any parent who is worried about their child's eating. The idea for it arose from a booklet we wrote some years ago addressed to parents of children who attended our eating disorders clinic. The booklet proved so popular that we were encouraged to expand it and this Parents' Guide is the result. We hope that it will prove to live up to its title and truly act as a guide for parents through the difficult world of eating disorders.

The term 'eating disorder' can mean many different things to different people. We are all familiar with the tragic stories that hit the headlines: death from anorexia nervosa of promising young people who should have so much to live for. Eating disorders are often featured in magazine and newspaper articles, and a whole range of confusing terms and explanations are offered. Myths abound and it can be difficult to separate the facts from popular beliefs. In this book we try to be clear about what is and what is not known. We will not use terms like 'slimmer's disease' to describe anorexia nervosa, because this term is inaccurate and misleading. We will not be suggesting that you view your child's eating difficulty as a phase of awkward, stubborn, defiant behaviour that is best ignored until it goes away. We will not be looking to the worlds of fashion and fitness to provide a full explanation for your child's problems and, finally, we will not be suggesting that you are a bad parent.

It is clear that you are a concerned and interested parent because you have picked up this book. So what will we hope to do? Your child might have any of a number of different eating difficulties. She (or he) might simply be a bit fussy about food, or be fearful of certain foods, or be having difficulty trying new foods, or be restricting food intake, possibly to the point of serious weight loss, or has perhaps adopted bizarre or unpredictable eating patterns and other worrying behaviour. You might have picked up this book because you are feeling at the end of your tether, or you might be asking yourself whether your child's eating behaviour is actually quite normal and you are worrying unnecessarily. Whatever aspect of your child's eating behaviour is causing you concern, this book should help you to understand some of the more common reasons why problematic eating behaviours arise, and what you and others can do to manage the situation.

We hope to help you see a bit more clearly through the muddle of myths, popular beliefs and your own and others' anxieties to the positive things that you as a parent can do. Throughout the book we make reference to the importance of parents working together as a team. If you are a single parent this does not mean that you can't use some of the ideas and suggestions we make. The main point is that children and young people with eating problems need consistency in how their difficulties are managed by the adults around them. As a single parent, you could share some aspects of child care with a friend, another relative, a childminder, or another adult. Where we refer to two parents adopting a consistent approach, this can be read as two adults. If you are parents who have separated but continue to spend time with and share responsibility for your child, then, again, it will be very important to look at ways in which you can develop some consistency as parents in your child's best interests.

Although you can dip into any bit of the book that seems relevant to you and your child, we advise that you do read it through completely so that you can gain as full an understanding as possible of your child's eating problems and how best to help. We have tried to make it as reader-friendly as possible, and throughout have included examples from our practice to illustrate particular points. (To preserve confidentiality we have, of course, changed the names.) In addition, we have included a glossary of terms, a list of useful addresses to contact, and reference to other books that may be of interest. Although eating disorders do affect boys, they are generally much more common in girls, and for ease of reading we shall tend to refer to the person with the eating disorder as 'she' unless referring specifically to boys, and where there are clear-cut differences between boys and girls we shall clearly state these.

The poem on p. vi clearly illustrates the torment of a teenage girl with anorexia nervosa. In just a few words the poet conveys some of the distress felt by young people with eating disorders.

We hope that having read this book you will have a full understanding of your own child's distress and feel more able to help in overcoming the problem.

Acknowledgements

We wish to thank all the families with whom we have worked and our many colleagues (too numerous to mention by name) from whom we have learned so much over the years. Without their ideas and wisdom this book would not have been written.

Introduction

Esther was thirteen. She was doing well at school and had a group of good friends. She loved horse riding in her spare time. In the spring she told her parents that she was going on a diet, as she wanted to lose weight. She wasn't particularly overweight but a number of her friends had started dieting and she didn't want to be too different from them. Her parents weren't too worried at first. After all, she seemed to be cutting out 'unhealthy' foods. She was growing up into someone who took some pride in her appearance, and anyway, she probably wouldn't stick to the diet. But Esther did, and her weight began to go down. Her parents' attempts to put her off dieting had no effect. A month later, when she had lost about 2 kg (4.5 lb), she decided to become vegetarian. She said that eating meat was cruel. Her parents suspected that this was just a way of cutting out more foods, part of her mission to carry on losing weight, but Esther vigorously denied this, insisting that she was a vegetarian for moral reasons. She wouldn't discuss this or anything else related to her eating habits further.

Three months after first starting her diet, Esther had lost 5 kg (11 lb). She looked thin, pale and unwell. Despite this, she appeared to have a remarkable amount of energy and had taken up swimming and jogging in addition to her horse riding.

Joanne, aged eleven, was small for her age, dark haired and loved writing stories. Her sisters, one younger and one older, were both blonde and quite tall for their age. Recently Joanne had lost weight and had become obviously thin. Yet Joanne was convinced that she was fat and no amount of reassurance by her parents made any difference. She was absolutely certain that she was fat, useless and ugly.

Anna, fifteen, had seemed to be a perfectly happy and normal girl with no obvious problems. She appeared settled at school and had never been the sort of child who complained or made a fuss about things. Her parents were glad that they hadn't had the sort of problems with their daughter that they knew other parents had with teenagers. Anna's Mum and Dad realized something might be wrong during the summer holidays. They had been shocked to see Anna in her swimsuit. She had obviously lost a considerable amount of weight without them having noticed it before. Her parents thought it strange that neither of them had been aware that Anna had even been on a diet or had become particularly fussy about her food. They began to worry that she may have some serious illness or medical condition that was causing her to waste away. However, thinking about this further, her mother recalled that over the last couple of months Anna had taken to going to the bathroom immediately after every meal. She realized with shock and disbelief that Anna must have been making herself sick without anybody noticing.

Alex, fourteen, was very worried when his father had a month off work after a mild heart attack. His grandfather had died from heart disease when Alex was six, and he became very concerned that his father might die too. He decided that he must make an effort to stay fit and healthy so that he would not get heart problems too. He started doing a lot of exercise and cutting fat out of his diet. The exercise began to get out of hand with Alex running several miles daily and doing about 200 press-ups. His parents noticed a change in his mood if for any reason he couldn't do his exercise. On one occasion, when his parents wouldn't let him go out jogging, he became extremely angry then spent two hours running up and down the stairs.

Andrea's mother was cleaning out Andrea's room when she came across her diary. She knew she probably shouldn't read it but could not resist taking a peep. She was taken aback and upset to read: 'I'm bad, I'm useless, I'm a failure'; 'I can't stop thinking about food, there is nothing else to think about'; 'I'm a slob'; 'Why don't they get rid of me'. She had no idea Andrea felt like this.

Rachel, aged thirteen, announced that she didn't want to eat with her family any more and that from now on she'd be eating alone in her room. She said she thought it was disgusting that other family members ate meat and that no one had a right to force her to take part in something she considered to be morally wrong. Even when her mother cooked meals without meat, Rachel refused to join them, saying she preferred her own company at mealtimes, or that she had so much homework it was easier to eat upstairs, or that she couldn't stand her brother's lack of table manners. She always seemed to have some excuse. She enjoyed cooking though, and often prepared meals for the others. Her Mum noticed that she mostly cooked things that she didn't eat herself. Rachel seemed to have an endless list of reasons why she couldn't or shouldn't eat things and became so angry if anyone challenged her that it was often easier for everyone to let her do things her own way.

Kirsty was sixteen when she developed a chaotic eating pattern. She was dissatisfied with the way she looked and wanted to try to lose weight. She tried to cut out some meals altogether but became so hungry that she had to have snacks throughout the day. Sometimes she would feel so bad about doing this when she actually wanted to lose weight that she'd say to herself, 'Today's been a bad day so I'll just eat more now and start again tomorrow.' She started eating whatever she could find in the fridge, usually at the end of the day when her Mum and Dad were in bed. She denied doing this despite it being obvious to her mother that someone was taking the food and having been caught a couple of times in the kitchen late in the evening. In addition her mother found large quantities of sweet and chocolate wrappers hidden under Kirsty's bed.

These scenarios are illustrations of some of the ways in which parents first become aware that their child has an eating disorder. Parents generally experience a complicated mixture of feelings, which can include inadequacy, bewilderment, helplessness, frustration, anger and guilt. They often cannot understand what has gone wrong or why their child should be behaving so oddly. Is what they are seeing an illness or just problem behaviour? Previously their child may well have been happy, popular and problem-free; at least, so it has seemed. Typically, she has had many friends, has been successful at her schoolwork and other school activities, and has generally not been one to complain. There may have been some family stresses such as illness, the death of a relative, move of house, change or loss of job, or tensions between the parents, but often there does not appear to be anything that is obviously related to the changes parents observe in their child. Even if there have been some tensions it is often difficult to view these as so problematic that they could logically be seen to cause something as self-damaging as an eating disorder.

So parents are confronted by their young daughter seemingly determined to harm herself by starving herself, making herself sick or sometimes using other methods to lose weight such as use of laxatives, and perhaps exercising excessively. In addition, her personality seems to have changed. She is no longer the confident and outgoing girl she used to be, having become withdrawn, moody and generally very unhappy.

Such a situation can leave parents with many unanswered questions. You may have many questions in your mind yourself. It is often very difficult to try to understand why eating problems have arisen, and you may spend a long time trying to remember whether anything has happened that might account for the difficulties you and your child are struggling with. The problem is often that there is no simple explanation. In addition, things that are of great significance and importance to your child may seem trivial or not particularly noteworthy to you. (Incidentally, this is, of course, also true in reverse!)

The behaviours that accompany some types of eating disturbance are in themselves difficult to understand. If you don't have an eating disorder it is almost impossible to be able to imagine not eating when you are hungry, or what it feels like to be so consumed with guilt after eating a normal-sized meal that you have to go and make yourself sick. It is hard to agree with someone who complains of being fat when they are as skinny as a rake. These are not logical, easily understandable things.

You may feel perplexed by the changes in your child's character and wonder why she is no longer able to see things as she used to, or why you no longer seem to have the relationship with her that you used to. Often your child may push away your attempts to help and tell you it's you who has the problem, not her. If you have more than one child, you may be worrying about trying to make things fair, how to explain things to younger brothers and sisters. The eating disorder should not take over in the family and all children will continue to have needs. Yet it can be difficult to maintain a sensible balance of attending to everyone's needs when eating problems can exert such a powerful influence over the whole family.

If you have a head buzzing with unanswered questions you are likely to feel quite unsure about what you should be doing. You may have read that giving zinc supplements helps, or that hypnosis can make eating disorders disappear, but is that true? You may worry that battling away so clearly against your child's wishes may be doing more harm than good. You may disagree as parents about how the situation should be handled, and not know how to decide who is right. And often the biggest concern of all can be the question of whether your child is causing herself damage or harm by what she is doing.

In this book we try to address these and many other questions and concerns. Our aim is to try to make some sense of disorders that appear to have no logic to them and understandably cause immense concern and distress.

We know that being the parent of a child with an eating disorder is extremely stressful. Some years ago we conducted a survey, with the help of the Eating Disorders Association (see the list of useful addresses at the end of the book) to ask about parents' experiences of the treatment and support they had received regarding their children's eating disorders from centres across the UK. The results showed that the toll on mothers, in particular, was considerable. Over half the mothers who replied reported negative changes in themselves. They described loss of trust, increased feelings of guilt, sadness, anxiety, fear and anger. They wrote honestly about feelings of resentment towards the child with the eating problem, and some mentioned their own loss of interest in food or guilt around eating normally.

One mother of a daughter with anorexia nervosa wrote:

I have been changed irrevocably by her illness. I no longer have any ambitions or hope for the future of my children

. . . I feel I have let her down as a mother. I love her so much, as does her father, but she has told us that she hates us both. I tried so hard to make her happy and to nurse her through her illness, but I think she blames me, and maybe she is right.

Another, also the mother of a daughter with anorexia nervosa, wrote:

Her life is a nightmare, but I see inside the obsessive, darkened child, the sunny child I remember, and I know we can rescue her. Tonight she told me that she knows it is difficult to be a parent to her now. I looked at her hollow eyes and thin skull and I hugged her and told her that it was all right, and that she would be getting better soon.

Thankfully, it is not as difficult as this for all parents, but we fully recognize that parents carry the heaviest load of anxiety and hard work in the task of helping children with eating disorders and other eating difficulties to put their problems behind them. Acknowledging this has been important in prompting us to write this book.

Before moving on, we thought it might be helpful to outline briefly the book's contents. In Chapter 1 we define and describe in detail the different types of eating disorders and eating problems that can affect children and adolescents. We make a distinction between normal and abnormal eating patterns, and try to clarify the differences between mild and serious problems.

Chapter 2 deals with what we know about the development of eating disorders, what the possible contributory factors might be and how they can work together to 'tip' someone into an eating disorder. Also, we look at what can keep the disorder going once it has developed.

In Chapter 3 we go through the most common signs and symptoms of the eating disorders, including the things that are normally hard to observe such as hiding food and being sick in secret. The aim of this chapter is to help parents become aware of what they should look out for and to help them decide whether or not their child may have an eating disorder.

The most important people in the management of a child's eating disorder are the parents, and Chapters 4 and 5 contain a step-by-step guide on how to help your child.

Chapter 6 aims to help parents decide when to seek professional advice, to whom they should turn, and what they might expect.

Parents have understandable worries about whether their child's eating disorder will ever go away and what harm, if any, might have been done. In Chapter 7 we describe what can happen in the course of the eating disorder, talk about ways of limiting longer-term damage, and look at prognosis – that is, whether people can get well and what makes them more likely to do so.

Throughout the book we have added the stories of some of the many hundreds of children and adolescents and their families that we have seen and treated over the years, to illustrate various points we are trying to make. In Chapter 8 we give more detailed examples with full case histories, so that the reader can follow the process of the eating disorder from its start through to recovery and staying well.

We end the book by drawing attention to some useful books and self-help manuals that have been prepared for people with eating disorders, their families and friends. We also provide details of various support organizations for people with eating disorders and their families.

If correctly managed, the majority of eating disorders do resolve. We hope that this book will prove to be an easily readable and practical guide for parents in helping their children to return to sustained, normal and robust health.

What are eating disorders?

There is a wide range of eating patterns in childhood and adolescence. Only a few of these are really problematic and most would not constitute an 'eating disorder'. Many children's eating patterns cause concern to their parents at some stage and yet these are usually just normal phases of development. For example, most toddlers go through a phase of food faddiness during which they will eat only a very narrow range of foods, possibly just three or four different foods. As long as they take in enough calories to avoid feeling hungry, and are growing normally, they are eating adequately. No harm comes to them and the vast majority will move on to normal eating in due course. A few children persist with their faddiness over the years and we will discuss these later in this chapter (see Selective Eating, p. 15).

Many children in their pre-school years go through a phase of quite restricted eating. Not only may the range of foods be narrow but also the amount eaten is small. It is surprising how such children manage to thrive because they seem to defy conventional wisdom about calorie requirements. In general, adults need to balance calorie intake with calorie expenditure to maintain a steady weight. Children need to take in more calories than they use up as they need the extra to grow. Yet some pre-school children really do seem to have an inadequate intake. Despite this they seem to have far more energy than their parents and are clearly not experiencing any harm. Again, this pattern tends to resolve with time and only a few children persist with such restricted eating (see Restrictive Eating, p. 18).

Another phase worthy of mention is that noted in many adolescents, during which they eat vast quantities of food. Indeed, at times they hardly seem to stop eating; having just finished one meal they launch into a large snack, which is repeated just before starting another meal, and so on. The two snacks do not interfere with the next meal. This is again usually simply a phase, presumably linked to the adolescent growth spurt when many more calories are required. This normal adolescent behaviour differs from that seen in some children who persistently overeat *throughout* their childhood. Almost always such children are overweight. We discuss this group below (see Compulsive Overeating, p. 21).

The examples given above represent the varying patterns of eating seen during childhood and adolescence, none of which is in itself abnormal or harmful. It is understandable that parents often become concerned about something as fundamental as their child's eating habits. Is she getting enough of the 'right' sorts of food? Is he eating too much or too little? Such concerns can be picked up by the child and may in some cases contribute to the continuation of difficult or worrying behaviour that might otherwise have been short-lived or unproblematic. As a general rule, if children are growing as expected and seem generally healthy and settled, variations in diet and eating patterns should not be a reason to worry.

What, then, constitutes a real cause for concern and, specifically, when does difficult eating become an eating disorder? In fact, the terminology is quite confusing because often eating disorders have as much to do with a negative and distorted view of oneself as with food and eating. People with eating disorders tend to be very critical of themselves, thinking that they are useless or not particularly worthwhile. This self-disparagement manifests itself through dissatisfaction with appearance, shape and size, and this dissatisfaction in turn leads to eating behaviour, which becomes problematic. This is already beginning to sound quite complicated, so let's take a step back and consider in turn the specific eating problems of childhood and adolescence. (The feeding problems of infancy and the pre-school years do not fall within the remit of this book and parents who have concerns about these are referred to the Further Reading section at the end of the book.) The conditions which we will discuss are:

- anorexia nervosa
- bulimia nervosa
- selective eating
- restrictive eating
- food phobia
- food avoidance emotional disorder
- compulsive overeating

Anorexia nervosa

Anorexia nervosa is perhaps the best known of the eating disorders. The term actually means 'nervous loss of appetite' but this is misleading because people with anorexia nervosa do not have a true loss of appetite; indeed they may have good appetites. The disorder is characterized by a strong drive to lose weight, and children with anorexia nervosa develop an ability to override and block out their feelings of hunger. This seems quite extraordinary to most people, as satisfying hunger pangs is a basic human instinct. People with anorexia nervosa will avoid eating whenever they can, and when eating is unavoidable they will try to eat as little as possible either in real terms or in calorific value. Because hunger does not disappear, the temptation to eat can sometimes be so strong that the young person 'gives in'. She will then feel dreadful for having done so, and there can be an overwhelming need to get rid of what has just been eaten. This can lead to the girl making herself sick, taking laxatives or exercising excessively. If a girl's periods had started before she developed anorexia nervosa, they will stop (we return to this in Chapter 3).

Anorexia nervosa is sometimes inappropriately called the 'slimmer's disease'. This is also misleading because it is not simply an extreme form of slimming or dieting somehow 'gone wrong'. Although these behaviours share the aim of losing weight, the vast majority of people who go on a diet do not develop anorexia nervosa. It is not just about 'successfully' restricting food intake; this is certainly a key aspect but one that overlies deeper problems and concerns such as an intense fear of gaining weight and getting fat, a very distorted view of one's body and the general self-disparagement we have already mentioned.

Susie, aged eleven, liked looking at her mother's magazines and carefully read all the tips about health and beauty. She began to feel unhappy with the way her own body looked compared to the pretty models she saw in the magazines and decided that she should put a bit more effort into losing some weight and staying healthy. She announced that she was too fat and was going to go on a diet. Her parents didn't take this too seriously at first, Susie looked fine to them, and they thought she probably would not be able to stick to a diet anyway. They began to get a bit annoyed at the way Susie insisted on choosing all the food for family meals and participating in their preparation. She became so angry and upset when her mother tried to stop her, or cooked something when Susie was out, that her parents began to get quite worried. It seemed easier for everyone to let her do what she wanted as no one in the family liked the shouting and arguing that was beginning to happen every evening. Susie would enthusiastically help serve the meals but ate very little herself. She began to make negative remarks about herself as a person, and about her body in particular. She started weighing herself two or three times a day. Her parents' attempts to reassure her and to encourage her to eat more led to tantrums and tears, with Susie screaming that she was already too fat and that she felt disgusting. She started losing weight quite rapidly. Nothing Susie's parents did or said seemed to help and eventually, feeling completely helpless, they sought help from their family doctor.

It can be seen from this example that Susie had far more of a problem than just dieting or 'slimming'. 'Normal' dieters stop dieting once they have lost some weight or, more usually, once they have got fed up with being on a diet; they certainly do not suffer from the very poor self-image so characteristic of people with anorexia nervosa. Susie manifested the characteristic features of an eating disorder, namely an extreme preoccupation with weight and shape, a distorted view of her body and a very poor view of herself, in addition to abnormal or inadequate eating. She genuinely believed she was fat and saw herself as overweight and disgusting, despite having lost a worrying amount of weight, and was extremely fearful of putting on more weight. In other words, abnormal eating is only one aspect of an eating disorder. People with anorexia nervosa often have perfectionist tendencies. They are inclined to set themselves high standards, which they work hard to achieve. Susie showed many of the features of childhood-onset anorexia nervosa.

Anorexia nervosa usually develops in girls and young women between the ages of fifteen and twenty-five, at an estimated rate of around one in every 200 females in this age group. However, it can also occur in children; the youngest we have seen with true anorexia nervosa being only seven years old. Although this is rare, we are no longer surprised when we do see such young children with this worrying problem. It occurs far more often in girls, with fewer than 5 per cent being boys. These children come from all different kinds of families in terms of race, religion, wealth and parental occupation.

It will be evident from Susie's story that anorexia nervosa is an illness that can seem to have little logic. People with anorexia nervosa think they are fat when they are thin, full when they are empty, failures when they are successful, useless, when they are useful, obsessed with food but avoid it, and see many advantages to being very thin despite all the dangers. It can be helpful to be aware that this apparent lack of logic is part of the illness and cannot be easily changed by normal reasoning. The child with anorexia nervosa will truly believe she is fat, ugly and useless, however unlikely or ridiculous that may seem to everyone around her.

Bulimia nervosa

The other well-recognized eating disorder is known as bulimia nervosa. 'Bulimia' means 'ox hunger' and refers to the fact that people with bulimia nervosa appear to have ravenous appetites. This is manifested by their tendency to engage in frequent binges, feeling they have lost control and eating quantities of food at one time that a 'normal' eater would consider to be excessive. During such episodes they may consume three or four times as much food as most people would eat in one meal, or sometimes even more. They may eat unusual combinations of things, such as peanut butter and ice cream, or they may eat large quantities of the same thing, for example two packets of chocolate biscuits. They feel deeply guilty and disgusted with themselves and almost always try to get rid of the food by making themselves sick. Occasionally, they may also use laxatives or other pills in an attempt to control weight gain, or they might try to go for long periods of time without eating anything at all. People with bulimia nervosa have the same deep-seated dissatisfaction with themselves as those with anorexia nervosa. They share a preoccupation with their weight and shape and judge their self-worth by the way they think they look. They are usually extremely self-critical in this respect and suffer from feelings of worthlessness. People with bulimia nervosa are often of normal weight, so their eating difficulties may be less apparent to the onlooker than is the case with the obvious weight loss accompanying anorexia nervosa, or their weight may go up and down more than is usual. In girls who have started menstruating, periods may become irregular or may stop altogether.

Fran, fifteen, had always been an outgoing, gregarious and somewhat impulsive girl. She started going out with boys when she was thirteen and had occasionally found herself in difficult situations. She also started experimenting with drugs and frequently drank alcohol. Her parents had been unaware of any of this, despite keeping what they believed to be a close eye on her. One night her mother found her sitting on the floor in the kitchen with the light off, eating food straight out of the fridge. When her mother asked what on earth she was doing, Fran ran upstairs screaming at her mother to mind her own business. She locked herself in the bathroom, where her mother could hear her retching and vomiting. Fran's mother felt confused and frightened; she did not understand what was happening to her daughter. Fran eventually emerged from the bathroom looking pale and unwell and they went downstairs to talk things over. She admitted that she had been doing this for several weeks, that the episodes occurred mostly when she was feeling upset, and that she absolutely hated herself.

Many young people with bulimia nervosa behave in ways similar to Fran. They worry intensely about their weight and shape, try hard to diet but binge regularly, feeling they have no control over these episodes. They then use vomiting, laxatives or exercising to control their weight, and sometimes a combination of all three. This can be very dangerous indeed (see Chapter 3). They differ from those with anorexia nervosa in that they tend to maintain their weight at a relatively normal level, or may sometimes be overweight. Young people with bulimia nervosa may not, on the surface, have the perfectionist tendencies commonly associated with anorexia nervosa and they may be more likely to engage in risk-taking behaviours such as experimenting with drugs, excessive drinking and unprotected sex. Almost always, these behaviours are related to feelings of self-dislike and being out of control.

Bulimia nervosa is rare before puberty and we have seen very few such children. However, once into adolescence the incidence increases and it probably affects around 3–4 per cent of teenage girls; it is rarer in boys, but does occur.

Selective eating

'Selective eater' is a term used to describe a child who will only eat a very restricted range of foods. Such children seem not to outgrow the normal developmental phase of food faddiness seen in younger children. They persist in eating only a very narrow range of foods, often as few as five or six. These foods tend to be carbohydrate based, although there may be some variation. Such children are averse to trying new foods and cannot usually be persuaded to do so under any circumstances. They may retch or appear to be going to be sick when confronted with new foods, although they clearly have no difficulty at all swallowing and keeping down their preferred foods. Surprisingly, they tend to thrive, usually being of normal height and of a reasonable weight. However, in some cases, particularly in children with long-standing, markedly restricted diets, weight may be higher or lower than normal, depending on the constituents of the diet. In general though, selective eaters do manage to obtain adequate calories, and the fact that they are generally healthy suggests that they are obtaining all the necessary nutrients. Even though at first glance their diets may appear rather unhealthy, most selective eaters will take sufficient amounts of the major food groups. There is sometimes a history of a close relative having had similar problems in childhood.

Sometimes selective-eating problems form part of a wider pattern of behaviour. A few children are very resistant to new experiences of any kind, preferring instead to stick to what they know. Such children do not like their routine to be disrupted, find new faces and places difficult to tolerate, or may become distressed at having to wear new clothes. They also find it difficult to make friends. These behaviours form part of a spectrum of behaviours associated with autism, autistic tendencies and Asperger's syndrome. Selective eating can sometimes be a reflection of the insistence on sameness and absence of risk-taking behaviour associated with this spectrum. If you think your child might fit into this spectrum, don't hesitate to consult your doctor to discuss your concerns further.

Medical investigations of selective eaters rarely reveal anything unusual or any underlying problems and these children usually tend to function quite normally in other respects. They do not seem to have any more problems than other children, although they can sometimes experience difficulties with friendships. Unlike children with anorexia and bulimia nervosa, they are not preoccupied with their weight and shape, do not have distorted views about their own body size and do not suffer from particularly low self-esteem. Most commonly it is the parents who are concerned about growth and social development. We usually see such children between the ages of about seven and eleven, when they are beginning to mix more with other children and the parents are worried not only about their health but also about the social implications of such narrow eating.

Younger children can usually get away with faddy eating habits but as school and social eating become more a part of life, the selective eater may become more isolated socially.

Rosie, eight, would eat only peanut-butter sandwiches, French fries, crisps, bananas and baked beans, and she would only drink water and chocolate milk shakes. She had stuck to the same foods for a number of years and was even particular about different brands of the same food. Her mother knew what to buy and her older brother and sister were so used to her fussy eating that they no longer noticed it. Rosie's grandmother and aunt had frequently expressed their concern in family discussions and although Rosie's parents agreed that it wasn't right, they really did not know what to do. Every time they tried something new, Rosie became very upset and said she was going to be sick. Despite trying every way they could think of to encourage Rosie to eat a wider range of foods, her parents had not had any success at all. Despite this she was growing normally, was not underweight and was otherwise happy and contented. She was doing well at school and had many friends. Rosie's parents finally sought help after she had spent a tearful weekend at the prospect of going to a school friend's house for tea and had refused an invitation to stay overnight with her best friend. Rosie's eating habits were now clearly interfering with her social development, stopping her from participating in activities that other girls of her age would normally enjoy.

This is a fairly typical manifestation of selective eating. The main problem is often the social restriction imposed, which often leads to a request for help. Having now seen a large number of such children and followed their development, we have concluded that in the majority of cases this condition is relatively harmless and certainly does not constitute a threat to health. These children tend to increase their range of foods as they enter their teenage years, possibly under the influence of peer-group pressure. Indeed, until quite recently we used to teach that all selective eaters grew out of it by the time they became adults. However, one of us (BL) was giving a lecture on selective eating and stated that *all* selective eaters grew out of it before adulthood. After the lecture a 27-year-old man, broadly built and very tall, introduced himself and told the speaker he was wrong. The man concerned had been a life-long selective eater (cheese crackers, Marmite sandwiches, French fries, potato crisps, spam and baked beans, now liberally diluted by beer most evenings) and, despite his mother's continuous anxiety about his health throughout his childhood and teenage years, had played rugby for his school and later the local club, and was also a black belt at judo. (BL apologized for his error!)

Restrictive eating

A number of children seem to fail to grow out of the phase of restrictive eating mentioned in the Introduction, when they simply seem not to eat very much at all. Their diet may be reasonably well balanced, and when they eat they do so in a normal way. However, they seem to have tiny appetites or not to be at all interested in food. Again, as with selective eating, there is no preoccupation with weight or body shape, no distorted view about body shape, and in general there are normal levels of self-esteem. Whereas it is common in the pre-school years, and apparently harmless, it can be more problematic if it persists for several years. Although restrictive eating appears to be a relatively uncommon condition, it is certainly one that understandably causes considerable concern, particularly when it has an impact on growth.

Dan had never really seemed to enjoy food. During his toddler years he ate relatively small amounts compared with his brother and sister. The family doctor suggested it was just a phase and that he would grow out of it. When he entered school he was noted to be shorter and thinner than his peers, and was seen by a paediatrician for tests. Nothing abnormal was found and he was referred to a dietitian for advice. Carefully constructed meal plans had no substantial effect. By the age of ten he was slightly shorter than average for age and very skinny. He ate very small portions but would snack frequently. There was no indication of any other problems.

Children like Dan do cause considerable anxiety. However, the majority do not seem to be seriously harmed by their inadequate diet. So far as we can tell they grow to be normal but skinny adults, who also eat poorly. Presumably they have different nutritional requirements from others, with perhaps a different metabolism. However, it is important to ensure that there are no associated emotional problems. Some children generally eat poorly because they are unhappy, worried or distressed in some way. We discuss this further below (see Food avoidance emotional disorder, p. 20). Also, when the problem has not been long-standing, but represents a relatively recent change in eating habits, it may be that there is a loss of appetite associated with depression. It is also important to distinguish this kind of restricted eating from what is known as 'failure-to-thrive'. This is a term usually applied to babies and children who do not grow as expected, often because of the lack of a strong positive emotional environment. Such children usually show a wide range of worrying behaviours, over and above poor eating. Don't hesitate to contact your doctor if you are in doubt.

Food phobia (sometimes known as functional dysphagia or fear of swallowing)

A number of children seem to be generally fearful of eating, and particularly of solid or lumpy foods. This is quite different from anorexia nervosa in which there is a major fear of weight gain. Children with food phobia avoid food not because they are preoccupied with their weight or shape or want to lose weight but because they are afraid of the food itself. Most children with food phobia are frightened of putting food in their mouths and swallowing it for fear of gagging, vomiting, choking or being poisoned.

John, nine, had developed normally until he was six. He had always eaten well and was growing as expected. Around three years before his parents brought him to the clinic he had told his mother that he had a pain in his chest when he ate. His mother had been alarmed and had taken him to the family doctor, which led to the pain being investigated in hospital. This did not reveal any cause for John's pain, which nevertheless persisted and seemed to be really bothering him. It was eventually decided that he needed a test, which involved passing a tube into his stomach. The doctor who carried out the test was rather brusque and unsympathetic to John's anxiety about the procedure. In consequence, the whole episode proved very traumatic. John gagged, and felt sick and frightened. After the test, he refused to eat for several days, and thereafter would only eat soft and mushy foods and clear drinks. By the time he came to the clinic, this had been going on for nearly three years.

It is not uncommon for children with food phobia to have experienced some form of trauma but by no means are such episodes always as clear-cut as that affecting John. Sometimes a relatively mild incident can trigger a seemingly overwhelming, exaggerated and long-lasting reaction. Usually this occurs in children who have particularly sensitive personalities. Alternatively, some children make peculiar or illogical associations between events in their mind, which may lead to the fearful avoidance of some foods.

Food avoidance emotional disorder

This condition is not readily recognized by doctors and may be confused with anorexia nervosa or one of the emotional disorders such as depression or anxiety. Many children between the ages of about five and sixteen have difficulties with eating that do not warrant a diagnosis of anorexia nervosa, bulimia nervosa or their variants, nor belong to the other categories referred to above. These children usually have some emotional problems, such as sadness, worries or obsessionality, which interfere with their appetite and eating. They, too, do not have the preoccupations, concerns and distorted views about weight and shape found in children with anorexia and bulimia nervosa.

Josie, fourteen, had become sad and tearful following the death of a much-loved family pet, with disturbed sleep and loss of appetite. The family doctor advised that this was an understandable reaction and that it would pass. One month later she was eating only one-quarter of her normal amount and had lost over 4 lb (2 kg).

Josie showed signs of food avoidance emotional disorder. She was in distress but not suffering from an eating disorder or other form of illness. She had symptoms suggestive of depression but did not have all the features. Such situations are not at all uncommon in childhood and often lead to food avoidance. Of course, some children may actually suffer from depression. This is manifested not only by loss of appetite but also by sleep disturbance, poor concentration, tearfulness and a general sense of hopelessness. Such children will usually say they feel miserable and their body posture, slowness of movement, facial expressions and tone of voice reflect this. Your doctor should be able to advise on diagnosis and treatment.

Compulsive overeating

Some children overeat from an early age and persist in this pattern throughout their childhood and adolescence. Parents often note that they seemed to have ravenous appetites even in infancy. Attempts to enforce diets rarely succeed and such children are invariably overweight. (If they are not then there is nothing to worry about!) Many such children seem to eat whenever they appear to be distressed and this pattern has been described as comfort eating.

Jadine, aged ten, was 30 lb (14 kg) overweight. She seemed always to have had a large appetite. Her parents had frequently tried to impose diets and had sought the assistance of dietitians on several occasions. If denied food, Jadine would have tantrums and raid the food cupboard when her parents were not looking. A paediatrician could find no obvious cause for her problem. Her parents had been aware for some time that Jadine did not get on well with other children and that she often spent time alone, when she would continuously snack.

Compulsive overeating differs from bulimia nervosa in that such children do not have episodic binges followed by making themselves sick, using laxatives, or trying to get rid of the food in other ways. Rather, they consistently overeat, rarely or never purge and are not overly preoccupied by their weight and shape. In addition, they tend not to experience the same sense of utter loss of control during their eating, nor the deep guilt and despair after eating. Unlike those young people with anorexia nervosa or bulimia nervosa, they make little or no effort to control their weight and may not express dissatisfaction with their size or shape. However, they do have in common with those with bulimia nervosa a tendency to eat and overeat when distressed. Compulsive overeating is equally common in boys and girls, and may affect as many as 5 per cent of the childhood population; it tends to run in families.

It can be seen from this overview of eating problems in childhood and adolescence that there is quite a wide range of disorders and that they all have in common abnormal eating patterns and underlying difficulties. In the next chapter we discuss what is known about the causes of these disorders.

What causes eating disorders?

One of the most common questions asked about an eating disorder is 'Why did she get it?' Unfortunately, this also happens to be one of the most difficult to answer. Although there is quite a lot of information about eating disorders once they have developed, no one completely understands why or how eating disorders occur. Certainly there are a number of factors that have to occur in combination before an eating disorder emerges. In other words, there is not one single cause, but underlying causes which are complex and multiple. We will now try to clarify what is known and identify those areas that need further understanding.

When considering the causes of any problem, it can be helpful to divide them into the three 'P' factors: (i) predisposing; (ii) precipitating; and (iii) perpetuating.

Predisposing factors

This term refers to those factors that are a necessary precondition for a particular disorder to emerge. They are things already present in the individual or the environment before the eating disorder develops. They don't actually precipitate or trigger the problem but have to be present for any precipitating factors to have the specific effect of producing the disorder. A simple analogy may be helpful here. If we want to drive our car, we turn on the ignition, release the hand brake, put it into gear and press the accelerator. However, for this process to have the effect of making the car move, the car has to have an engine, wheels and many other parts. The engine and wheels are necessary preconditions for the car to start and move. Without them it does not matter how many times we turn on the ignition, release the hand brake and engage the correct gear, nor how vigorously we press the accelerator – the car will not start, let alone move. The engine and wheels are predisposing conditions (or factors).

Alternatively, we can turn to another more obviously related example. Some people are born with the sensitive lungs and airways characteristic of asthma. The same people may or may not develop breathing problems, depending on the environment they live in. For example, if an individual is brought up and lives in a large city, he may receive a diagnosis of asthma as a child and need to rely on inhalers to regulate his breathing for much of his adult life. However, if that same person was born and brought up in the Swiss mountains, for example, he might never develop breathing problems and so might never know he had the potential to develop asthma. In this example, the sensitivity of the lungs and airways are the predisposing factors.

Similarly, with the eating disorders (and many other illnesses) there are necessary predisposing conditions, without which any number and intensity of triggering or precipitating factors will fail to produce an eating disorder. So what are these predisposing conditions?

Genetics
Many people are surprised that genes may be important contributors to eating disorders. This is understandable given that only a minority (5–10 per cent) of people with eating disorders has a close relative with an eating disorder.

The question is, 'If a relative doesn't have an eating disorder, how can it be genetic?'

Genetic transmission of illness or predisposition to illness occurs in varying and usually complex ways. Only rarely is it as straightforward as 'one parent passing it on to a child'. Genetic transmission is determined by the contribution of both parents, and often there is a combination of genes contributing. The exact contribution of genes to the development of eating disorders and the mode of transmission is not yet fully understood. However, there is substantial evidence to show that genes are relevant.

One of the best ways of determining the contribution of genetic factors to any problem is to study the differences between identical and non-identical twins. This is because identical twins have an identical genetic make-up, whereas non-identical twins do not. In consequence, if genes are relevant to the development of a disorder, we would expect that when that particular disorder occurs in an identical twin, it would be much more likely also to occur in the other identical twin than to occur in a non-identical twin. In the case of anorexia nervosa occurring in a non-identical twin, the likelihood of it also affecting the other twin is about 5 per cent. In contrast, when an identical twin has anorexia nervosa, the chances of her sister also having it are around 56 per cent. It can be seen that when the genes are identical the chance of both twins having anorexia nervosa is increased ten-fold. The figures for other eating problems such as bulimia nervosa, selective eating and food avoidance emotional disorder are less clear, but it would be surprising if genes did not play some part.

An obvious question arises in relation to the twin studies. If identical twins share the same genes then why, when one twin has anorexia nervosa, do only around 56 per cent of siblings get it? Surely it should be 100 per cent? The answer lies in the fact that there are a number of factors, in addition to the genes, that all come together to create the problem. It is very, very unlikely indeed that only one part of one gene 'causes' eating disorders. It seems that the genes are a necessary condition, but only part of the whole. Nor is it yet fully understood how genes contribute to the development of eating disorders. It is possible that they operate through producing some of the other predisposing factors.

Let us therefore consider some of these. The two that are most likely to be genetically determined relate to personality and biological make-up.

Personality
It is well recognized that people with anorexia nervosa tend to have a somewhat conscientious and perfectionist

personality. They strive to do things to the best of their ability and will often apply themselves to tasks in an obsessional or driven manner. For example, they may spend hours on a particular piece of homework, often finding it hard to complete to their satisfaction. The same diligence is applied to most areas of their lives, and, compared with many of their peers, they tend to be unusually well-behaved and conforming young people. Indeed, parents often comment that prior to the onset of the anorexia nervosa they had never had a single worry about their daughter. Children like this can sometimes set themselves unrealistically high standards. When they don't achieve these peaks they may feel that they have failed, with an adverse effect on their self-esteem.

Although all these characteristics are not universal to all people with anorexia nervosa, they do appear to apply to the majority.

Sophie, aged twelve, increasingly made private rules for herself. These included keeping every last thing in its proper place in her bedroom, spending at least three hours on her homework each evening, and only allowing herself to watch two television programmes a week. She felt good sticking to her rules but worried that she should do better, and gradually made up more. At first Sophie's parents did not really notice anything. They saw her growing into a sensible, thoughtful girl who got excellent reports from school and did not make extra work for her mother – unlike her brother whose room was always a mess! Yet Sophie was not satisfied with her efforts and each day promised herself that she would try a little harder. If she did not do as well at school, or did not get as high a mark as she had hoped for, she felt she must be lazy and that she should work harder. As her negative view of herself grew, she eventually decided that she needed to pay more attention to her diet. She felt she was putting on too much weight and that she needed to control this.

The rest of Sophie's story is by now familiar – she went on to develop anorexia nervosa. Sophie had the type of personality that is often associated with anorexia nervosa. In other words, her personality predisposed her to its development.

In contrast, those with bulimia nervosa tend to be less conforming and perhaps generally more rebellious. Often they are quite impetuous, extrovert and gregarious individuals. It is not uncommon for them to engage in risk-taking behaviour, such as drug misuse, smoking, drinking and promiscuous or unprotected sex. In other words, they tend to have somewhat impulsive personalities, in contrast to the conforming and conscientious personality of the youngster with anorexia nervosa.

Helen, fourteen, had always been a popular, sociable girl. She had an older sister which made it easier for her to get her parents to agree to her going out to clubs and discos from a relatively early age. On Friday and Saturday nights Helen always went out with a group of friends. She drank alcohol, experimented with drugs and was popular with boys. Helen liked having a laugh and a good time with boys but did not feel comfortable with the idea of sex. Nevertheless, she had found herself in difficult situations on a number of occasions and had ended up doing more than she wanted. When this had happened she always felt terribly guilty and dirty. She thought that she must be a no-good sort of person, who probably deserved to feel bad. She began to drink more when she went out because she knew she would probably end up doing something she did not want to, and at least then she'd be able to give herself the excuse of being drunk. Helen began to feel bad about her behaviour and her body and found that making herself sick helped her to get rid of some of the bad feelings, at least for a short time.

Helen went on to develop bulimia nervosa. She had a very different personality to Sophie, one that led her more easily into chaotic, impulsive behaviour. In Helen's case, these characteristics predisposed her to the development of bulimia nervosa.

Children with the other types of eating problems, such as food phobia and selective or restrictive eating, tend to have quite sensitive personalities, generally seeming to find life harder than their contemporaries.

Luke, aged nine, had always been a rather shy, quiet child. He had found it difficult to settle at playgroup and, when he started school, he had been tearful and very reluctant to leave his mother. He did have some friends at school but seemed to prefer not to spend a lot of time with them outside school hours. He found a number of the children in his class quite intimidating and spent most of his time with the two boys he felt comfortable with. Luke was an only child who worried a lot about his parents' health and safety. He hated it when his father went away on business because he was frightened that he might have an accident and never come back. Luke began to worry about food. He had heard and seen things on the television about people becoming ill and even dying from infected food. He developed stomach aches after eating things he wasn't sure were safe. There were a few things he knew were all right because he did not feel ill after eating them. He decided to stick to these foods so that nothing bad would happen.

In Luke's case, his dietary restriction eventually became a real cause for concern and his mother took him to see the doctor. In this example, Luke's anxiety and sensitivity were the predisposing factors for the development of his eating problems. His personality type made it more likely that he would develop a phobic, restrictive eating problem than one of the other types of eating disorder.

It is important to emphasize that these are stereotypes and do not necessarily apply to all young people with a particular eating problem. Indeed, this could not be the case given that some with anorexia nervosa later develop bulimia and that others fluctuate between the two. However, the association between type of eating disorder and the tendency towards a particular personality type suggests that personality is a possible predisposing condition.

Although not strictly a personality characteristic, it is worth mentioning here the central role of poor self-esteem in the development of eating problems. Almost invariably, children with eating difficulties do appear to have a very poor view of themselves for a wide variety of reasons. Although it could be argued that this occurs as a consequence of the eating problems, this seems unlikely. In our experience, most children appear to have felt badly about themselves before the eating problems arose. It seems more likely that poor self-esteem contributes to the development of eating difficulties. As mentioned above, this poor self-image can relate to a failure to achieve self-imposed impossibly high standards. Such children are desperate to strive to better themselves and their achievements, often setting themselves unattainable goals. Exerting strict control over appetite, weight and shape can in itself become something to work hard at and can allow a sense of achievement, which becomes self-perpetuating.

Emily, eleven, had felt for a long time that she just wasn't good at anything. She had an older sister who everyone thought of as the brainy one in the family. Her sister always got excellent reports and all the teachers seemed to think she was wonderful. Emily also had a younger sister, Laura, who was nine and still at Emily's old school. Laura had blonde curly hair and was very pretty and vivacious. She always got a lot of attention and loved telling stories and jokes. Emily felt the odd one out, not clever and pretty like her sisters. There was nothing left for her to be best at. She decided to go on a diet as she was becoming alarmed at the way her body was changing. She lost a bit of weight and a few people commented on how nice she was looking. Emily thought that at last she had found something to be good at – sticking to a diet. She was determined to keep going, and did so.

Josh was thirteen and the youngest of three boys. His two brothers were much older than him and had left school. One was already making a success of a banking career and the other was a medical student. Josh knew his parents were very proud of them. Josh was at the same boarding school his brothers had gone to and was very worried that his parents expected him to be brilliant. He knew that he was reasonably OK at school but also that he had to work quite hard to keep up with the others. He was always in the bottom half of the class when it came to tests. He was also not a natural sportsman. He hated rugby and football, whereas both his brothers had been in the school team. The one thing Josh knew he was good at was being persistent. He decided to join the cross-country-running club at school and found he was quite good at it. Having won a race he became determined to make this the thing he could excel in. Josh worked increasingly hard at his training and altered his diet to be more fit and healthy. Unfortunately, he did not stop, and became quite obsessed with the need to keep his exercise levels up and his diet to a minimum.

Biological factors

There has been an enormous amount of research into the possibility of there being some form of biological abnormality that leads to the development of eating disorders. Possibilities that have been considered include:

- A delay in stomach emptying, that is, that in people who have eating disorders food stays in the stomach longer before passing down the digestive system, which in turn means that they tend to feel full for longer.
- Some defect in the endocrine system, in particular in the glands that act on appetite regulation through the secretion of various hormones.
- A deficiency in some vital nutrient such as zinc or magnesium.
- A minor fault in one small part of the brain that could lead to misleading messages being sent to the rest of the body (see below).

So far, research endeavours into finding a biological cause have not proved very productive. This is in part because we have not previously had the necessary technology to allow a full investigation of the finer details of brain functioning. Also it is very hard to know whether the various changes that have been identified in the body are *primary* (present before the eating disorder developed) and thus may have contributed to it, or whether they are *secondary* (due to the effects of the eating disorder, such as starvation, weight loss and vomiting). Each type of cause can lead to quite dramatic changes in the structure and functioning of different parts of the body.

To illustrate the difficulty in distinguishing primary from secondary aspects of the eating disorder, let us consider what happens to the ovaries in anorexia nervosa. From the use of ultrasound examination we know that when someone has anorexia nervosa their ovaries are much smaller than they should be for the person's age. They also have a different appearance, with fewer and smaller follicles than would normally be expected (see Chapter 6). The uterus is also much smaller than it should be, and its size and shape change back to those of a young child. Now the question that arises is whether these changes contribute to the anorexia nervosa or are an effect of it. We know from monitoring the ultrasound appearances as recovery commences and weight is regained that the ovaries and uterus start maturing, and that when normal weight has been achieved and maintained for a few months the ovaries and uterus return to normal. This suggests that the immaturity of the ovaries and uterus is likely to be secondary to the weight loss, rather than pre-dating and perhaps contributing to its onset.

A number of authorities have made vigorous claims for the role of zinc deficiency in causing anorexia nervosa. Although there is little doubt that most people with starvation are deficient in zinc (and, for that matter, many other essential nutrients), there is no evidence that the zinc deficiency seen in people with anorexia nervosa pre-dates the illness; rather, it appears that the deficiency is secondary to starvation. Therefore it cannot be said that low levels of zinc *cause* anorexia nervosa. However, it is possible that zinc deficiency perpetuates any loss of appetite, and this will be discussed further later (see Perpetuating factors, p. 39).

A similar explanation seems to apply to many of the findings of abnormalities or changes in people with anorexia nervosa. For example, brain scans of people with anorexia nervosa tend to show shrinkage of brain tissue. If this shrinkage were responsible for the weight loss then it would probably not reverse with weight gain. However, in most cases the appearances on brain scan tend to revert to normal once weight has been regained.

The situation is probably more complex than this with regard to the changes seen in a number of chemical processes in the body. Unlike many of the changes noted in people with anorexia nervosa, which are most likely to be a consequence of the disorder, the relationship between different chemical processes and eating behaviour is rather more difficult to tease apart. Our appetite and sense of fullness are governed by a very complex interaction between a number of different chemicals and messages travelling between the brain and the stomach. In healthy individuals, and even in the early stages of anorexia nervosa, messages are relayed to the appetite regulation centre conveying the need to eat or not as the case may be. However, even in previously healthy individuals, once starvation sets in, for whatever reason, the normal sequence of messages becomes disturbed, with a change in appetite, despite the need for food. It is probable that the sense of fullness experienced by people with established anorexia nervosa is a result of this paradoxical process. Their brains are confused by conflicting messages of hunger and fullness. It is probable that people with bulimia also experience misleading messages about hunger and feelings of fullness, often leading them to eat or crave food when they would normally be expected to feel full. The chemical processes that might lead to this paradoxical situation are yet to be understood, but there is some evidence that there is some abnormality in the chemical messenger system.

A further puzzle relates to the distortion in perception of body size that is so characteristic of anorexia nervosa and, to some extent, bulimia nervosa. Almost invariably the body, or parts of it, is seen as fat, when in reality it may be emaciated. There is no doubt that this distorted perception is genuine; there is no question of deceit and scientific studies have confirmed this misperception. It is highly likely that this arises from some abnormality of brain function, just as does the faulty appetite regulation. This whole area is very complex and many questions remain unanswered. It seems that, in general, hunger and satiety perceptions result from a combination of cognitive sets, external and internal physiological cues. Precisely how these interact to produce what occurs in eating disorders remains unclear.

Until recently there was an absence of sufficiently sophisticated techniques to investigate the complexities of brain structure and function. However, new developments in neuroimaging have made it possible to investigate in great detail the minutiae of brain structure and function. These are early days and there is much to be learned. A number of studies, from around the world, indicate that there are indeed abnormalities in brain functioning in people with eating disorders. In our own research into childhood-onset anorexia nervosa, we have found abnormal activity in a specific brain circuit, and this abnormality does not seem to reverse with weight gain. This particular area of the brain deals with sense of fullness, appetite and emotion regulation, and visual-image processing. As all of these are dysfunctional in anorexia nervosa, it is tempting to postulate that this abnormality could contribute to its causation. However, it may be that the abnormality persists in those who are not fully recovered. They may well have reached a healthy weight and been able to maintain this, but still have distorted thoughts and attitudes about their body weight and shape. The next few years will hopefully provide some answers.

Even less is known about the role of biological factors in the development of other eating problems. Almost certainly, restrictive eating and its opposite, compulsive overeating, have some biological determinants, as well as other external contributory factors. So far we have discussed the role of genes, personality and biology in the origin of eating problems. However, there is one other major area for our consideration.

Sociocultural factors
It is well recognized that the majority of eating problems, and particularly anorexia and bulimia nervosa, occur in societies where food is relatively plentiful. In those countries where food is scarce, eating disorders are extremely rare. However, it is interesting to note that when people migrate from less industrialized countries to more prosperous societies, they or their children may well develop eating disorders. This all points towards the contribution of sociocultural factors in the development of eating disorders. Indeed, it seems that living in a relatively prosperous society is a necessary precondition.

It is not too difficult to understand why this might be the case. In societies where food is scarce there is a tendency to value fatness as a sign of prosperity. In contrast, where food is plentiful, being overweight is regarded more negatively, viewed by many as unattractive, and often seen as a result of greed. Indeed, there is some evidence to show that overweight children are teased and mocked more than children with any other problem. In contrast, thinness tends to be over-valued, with society tending to uphold a slim body shape as something for women to strive for.

The most obvious manifestations of this are in the media and the fashion industry. Advertisements for a wide range of products, and not just clothes, tend to feature thin models. Very rarely is there use of normal-weight models, let alone the overweight. Furthermore, bookstalls and news-agents are full of magazines promoting slimming diets, the virtues of being thin and the covert message that for a woman to be successful she must be thin. Children are also exposed to these pressures and grow up in a culture promoting dieting behaviour and dissatisfaction with the normal variation in body sizes and shapes. In the presence of other predisposing factors mentioned in this chapter, such stresses may contribute to the development of an eating disorder.

Boys are now also under increasing pressure to con-form to a certain body image, the emphasis being on a firm toned shape, which is then equated with good health. Health and fitness concerns are extremely common in boys with anorexia nervosa, who will state that they are dieting and exercising to be healthy. In reality they are dieting and exercising to excess.

We should mention at this point the impact of public health campaigns and education on some individuals. We know that there is a tendency in most developed countries for up to a quarter of people to be overweight, even more than this in some countries. A lot of time, energy and money are invested in trying to encourage us to alter our eating habits as a whole, to promote better general health and to reduce illness and disease associated with being overweight. A good example of this has been the emphasis on not eating too much saturated fat because of the relationship between over-consumption of fats and heart disease. The education and advertising have been directed primarily at men, where the problem was identified as the greatest. These campaigns have been very successful at getting the message across, and most people are aware that you can 'look after your heart' by being careful with your diet. However, this message is intended for an adult, on average overweight, population. It is not intended for normally developing children. We have seen many boys, not overweight to start with, who have become extremely concerned about their fat intake and gradually eliminated fat from their diet. Worries about heart disease and other health-related concerns associated with diet are very common in boys with eating disorders. The health messages that our society as a whole needs to hear and act upon will, of course, not be appropriate for a number of people. However, such messages form part of the backdrop of information, pressures and advice that our children grow up with.

It is important to emphasize that societal pressure is just one of several necessary preconditions or predisposing factors that may contribute to the development of eating disorders. People sometimes think that sociocultural factors of the kind we have discussed cause the eating disorder. This is almost certainly not the case, but they do form the background against which eating disorders can more easily develop.

Precipitating factors

We now need to give consideration to the precipitating or triggering factors. These are the factors that seem to trigger the onset of the eating problem. They can only do so in the presence of the necessary preconditions discussed above. It is almost as if they represent 'the final straw', 'the straw that broke the camel's back'. They will be what tips the already vulnerable individual into the dieting behaviour or other change in eating patterns.

A common example in anorexia nervosa is that of the child who is teased at school for being slightly overweight, goes on a diet, and then develops anorexia nervosa. Her parents are likely to believe that it was the teasing that caused the illness. They are correct in that the teasing may indeed have precipitated the dieting that resulted in the problem but an eating disorder would not have developed in the absence of certain preconditions. Possibly there would be some other reaction or illness, for which there would be other preconditions. For example, if a child has a tendency to have asthma attacks (also genetically determined), then teasing about being overweight (or anything else) may precipitate an asthma attack. So it can be seen that the same trigger can have completely different consequences, determined by the preconditions.

There are many examples of precipitating factors for the eating disorders besides teasing. Indeed, any form of stress may be sufficient. Each person will differ in their reaction to different stressors and children who have gone on to develop eating disorders describe a very wide range of stressful events or situations. Examples include:

- forthcoming examinations
- poor peer-group relationships
- other difficulties at school
- changing school
- moving house
- the loss of a friend, relative, pet or other loved one
- family tensions
- severe traumas, such as witnessing an accident, being victimized or abused.

As many as one-third of adult women with eating disorders give a history of some form of adverse or unwanted sexual experience during childhood or adolescence. It is quite likely that a similar proportion of children and adolescents with eating disorders have had an uninvited, unwanted or adverse sexual experience. Sexual abuse of children does not necessarily occur within the context of the immediate family; indeed, more commonly the perpetrator is not a member of the immediate family.

Chloe, twelve, was becoming increasingly distressed by the changes in her body as she went through puberty. She did not want to have to wear a bra like some of the other girls in her class but her mother had said they should buy one soon. She did not want to grow up and, in particular, she did not want to have a woman's curvy body. She felt very jealous of her eight-year-old sister who was a real tomboy and didn't have to worry like she did about bras and periods and things. Chloe thought that she might be able to avoid things by going on a diet. That would allow her to keep her legs thin and her chest flat like her sister. Chloe started cutting down and eventually went on to develop anorexia nervosa.

It was only after she had been in treatment for nearly a year that she felt safe enough to indicate that she had had a very bad experience. Chloe eventually managed to reveal that she had been sexually abused by a lodger who had been living in the house with her family. He had stayed less than a year but during this time had built up a friendship with her, which turned into him engaging in inappropriate sexual contact with her over a number of months. He had made Chloe promise never to tell anyone at all and although she thought what was happening was wrong, she had been frightened to say anything because she thought he would find out. When he had left, she had tried hard to forget all about it and thought it must have been her fault. She knew that as she grew older and began to look more like a woman, other boys and men would start looking at her. She hated the idea of this and knew that she must avoid it at all costs. Eventually, Chloe was able to share what had happened with her mother and she gradually acknowledged that what the lodger had done was not her fault. It took a long time for Chloe to feel more comfortable with her body and its changing shape.

Marie, thirteen, lived in a village where she had a number of good friends. Every Friday evening one of their fathers would take it in turn to take them to the youth club in the neighbouring village. At first, Marie really enjoyed going. They danced and had good fun, and she met some new friends. A group of older boys started coming and one of them became very friendly with her. At first she felt very flattered because she knew he was twenty. He lived near the hall where the youth club was held and he and Marie started going to his flat instead. When they were there, he seemed to change and become a different person. He made Marie undress him and touch him in a way that she didn't feel comfortable with. He told her that she shouldn't tell anyone at all as it had to be their secret, and he always took her back to the hall in time to be collected. Each time he made her swear that she would be there again the next Friday.

Marie began to get more and more frightened by his behaviour but he knew where she lived and had threatened to set the house on fire if anyone ever heard about it. Marie's friends often asked where she kept disappearing to on Friday nights and why she always seemed so quiet now. Marie felt more and more disgusted with herself and what she did on Fridays. She dreaded the end of the week and, when she got home on Friday night, always went to the bathroom to be sick. She found this made her feel better and over the next few months developed a chaotic pattern of eating and making herself sick. She ended up looking so ill that her mother took her to the doctor.

Perhaps the most common of the precipitating factors in anorexia nervosa is the advent, or recent onset, of puberty, with all the accompanying anxieties and complications of changing body, emerging sexuality, peer-group pressure and struggle for independence while still emotionally relatively immature.

Children are very aware of the physical and emotional changes they experience at this age, such as the development of an adult body shape, frequent mood swings and, for girls, menstruation. Such changes are inevitable and largely out of their control. The normal physical changes of puberty are often also accompanied by anxiety about adolescent and adult behaviour and expectations. A whole range of issues needs to be confronted, and many young people have worries and concerns about things that they will not have needed to think about until now. What do I do about drugs? What if my friends get drunk? How do I handle boys? Is it OK to like being with my Mum and Dad or does it mean I'm boring? I'm not sure I like hanging around in the cafe with my friends, but they'll think I'm sad if I don't. All these questions and worries can lead some children to feel very out of control and to search for an area in their lives where they can exert control. In many adolescents this may be over clothes – insisting on wearing striking or unusual items; or it could be over their rooms – insisting on decorating them in a way that does not coincide with parental taste! Such expressions of independence and self-identity are normal and usually harmless; they represent a method of exerting some control and give a sense of achievement. Indeed, they are a very necessary part of growing up with the testing out of expressions of individual wishes and personal style often first being done in the relative security of the family.

However, some children try to exert the same control over what they eat; restricting food intake is for them a sign of successful control. It can in some cases seem as if there is very little else that they can be in charge of in the same way. They may at first receive positive comments about their healthy eating or the fact that they are taking more exercise than before. They may lose a bit of weight and hear people commenting on how well they look, or sense their friends' jealousy. The good feeling that weight loss produces, and the sense of control that goes with it, may encourage continued dieting. If then they give in to the urge to eat they feel out of control, so they work harder to avoid eating and to lose weight. Herein lies the downward spiral into an eating disorder. This sequence applies especially to those children with perfectionist tendencies, who already have a sense of failure as a result of not being able to achieve their impossibly high self-imposed standards. Although puberty is not necessarily a risk factor for the emergence of bulimia nervosa, a similar process occurs. However, those with bulimia nervosa are less able to maintain control and often experience a sense of loss of control accompanied by bingeing.

The other eating problems – selective eating, restrictive eating, food phobia, food avoidance emotional disorder, and in some cases compulsive overeating – all tend to start prior to puberty. Clear precipitants may be hard to identify. However, food phobia is quite likely to be precipitated by a traumatic episode such as that experienced by John, described in Chapter 1. This association between eating or swallowing and some form of trauma is commonly found in food phobia. The other conditions often have an insidious onset and it may be hard to pinpoint the starting point, let alone any precipitants. If and when these can be identified, they are likely to be different between individuals.

It is often quite difficult to do much about the predisposing and precipitating factors, which is why it is so important to give careful consideration to the third 'P', the perpetuating (or maintaining) factors.

Perpetuating factors

Once the eating problem has developed, any precipitating factors that persist are likely to contribute to its maintenance. For example, if teasing or academic pressure has played a part in precipitating an eating problem, and this stress continues, then it is very likely also to maintain the eating difficulty.

Jonathan, twelve, was the oldest of four children. He was the only boy, with three younger sisters. His father was a university professor and his mother was a lawyer. His aunts and uncles all had successful, well-paid careers. It sometimes seemed to Jonathan that his family was so clever that he could never do as well. His father had attended a well-known independent school as a boy and Jonathan's name had been on the waiting list of the same school since soon after his birth. Jonathan knew you had to be very clever to pass the exams to get in and really wasn't at all sure that he would make it. He also knew that it would mean a lot to his father for him to go to the same school and he desperately did not want to disappoint him. After all, he was the only son, so his father wouldn't have another chance. From about the age of eleven Jonathan began to worry about the big exam looming before his thirteenth birthday. In the meantime he had tests at the end of each term, which he increasingly dreaded. He tried very hard to do well at his schoolwork and spent long hours doing his homework. His parents worked long hours too and his sisters seemed always to be at dancing or music classes or with friends after school. Try as he might, he never seemed to get anything more than average marks. Jonathan increasingly thought that he must be lazy and stupid and decided to be a bit stricter with himself in as many ways as he could. That way he might do better in the end-of-term exams a few weeks away. He made sure he didn't eat too much, and was careful to avoid anything that might seem as if he was treating himself. He thought that he didn't deserve biscuits and chocolate, or other things that used to be his favourite foods. The end-of-term exams came and went with the usual results. Jonathan felt that he had failed and promised himself that he would keep an even tighter check on himself from now on. He wanted to feel completely on top of things in time for the big exam at the end of the year.

In Jonathan's case, academic pressures contributed to the development of what later became full anorexia nervosa. These pressures persisted and contributed to the maintenance of his eating difficulties.

However, it is also perfectly possible that other factors, which arise as a result of the eating disorder, maintain it. To understand this process better it might be helpful to picture a child kicking a football on a level piece of land. Unfortunately, the ball rolls over the edge of a hill and drops out of the child's reach. The child was responsible for initiating the football's movement but is no longer able to influence it. None the less, the football continues to move under the influence of gravity. So the child was the precipitating factor in initiating the ball's movement but gravity perpetuates it.

There are many examples of this process. Many girls who go on a diet are told how good they look as they start losing weight. This gives them a sense of well-being, which encourages them to continue dieting. As they lose more weight, they experience a strong sense of comfort, control and achievement, each of which contribute to their feeling good about themselves. This enhanced sense of well-being perpetuates the process as they have no wish to give up such a good feeling.

Trina, aged fourteen, had lost 9 kg and was very underweight. She said that she liked her new appearance and felt very proud of herself for losing so much weight. She had no wish to regain the lost weight believing that she couldn't possibly feel so good as she did now.

Trina's strong sense of well-being perpetuated the illness. Another illustration of perpetuating factors is given by the case of John in Chapter 1, who had a fear of swallowing following a traumatic hospital procedure. His parents were actually very understanding, sympathetic and supportive. They eagerly sought and carried-out advice on how to help John overcome his fears, with early success. However, had they taken a different approach, for example forcing John to eat or punishing him if he didn't, it is more than likely that John's difficulties would have been perpetuated. In other words, his parents' behaviour would have acted as a perpetuating factor.

The bad and the good news for parents is that their response to their child's eating problems does often serve to perpetuate the difficulty. This is obviously bad news because no one wants to be responsible for maintaining a problem, however inadvertent this may be. And in almost all cases this does occur inadvertently.

Ben, aged nine, was a selective eater whose narrow range of accepted foods included one particular brand of white sliced bread. His mother always made sure the freezer was well stocked because whenever she had tried to get Ben to try a different sort of bread, she, Ben and her husband had all ended up arguing, shouting and crying. Ben's mother hated upsetting Ben, as he was a thoughtful, good boy and it didn't really seem too much trouble to make sure he had what he liked in the house. Unfortunately, Ben's mother suddenly became very ill, and had to go into hospital for a week. Her husband took time off work to look after Ben and his younger sister. His mother knew that she had left plenty of Ben's food and on the day before she was due to return home had written the shopping list for her husband. He drove her home the next day after receiving instructions from the hospital to make sure his wife rested for the next few days. When they got home she discovered that he had bought the wrong type of bread and that there would be nothing for Ben's packed lunch the next day. Ben's Dad thought it was time they stopped giving in to Ben all the time. After all, he'd bought some white sliced bread and anyway all the shops were closed except for a late-opening supermarket five miles away. Again, they had an argument about it, which ended up with Ben's mother driving to buy a loaf herself even though she knew she was supposed to be taking things very slowly having just come out of hospital.

However, the fact that parents may inadvertently perpetuate their child's eating problems is also good news because it means that if they are aware of the effects of their behaviour, they can do something about this themselves. Certainly they may need help, but at least there is a readily accessible potential for change. In the above example, Ben may well have been persuaded to try the different bread just for one day. He had never been presented with a real opportunity to try other foods because his mother went to such great lengths to supply him with the very narrow range of foods he would accept. The above situation could have been an ideal chance for Ben to try something very slightly different and, if he achieved this, it might have helped him to continue to try new things.

The following examples all illustrate ways that perpetuating factors can be changed, thus allowing the children to move away from their eating disorders.

The parents of Laurie, fifteen, were unable to agree on how best to deal with her anorexia nervosa. Her father took a very firm line, using coercion and threats. In contrast, her mother preferred a much gentler approach using cajoling and promises of rewards. They continued over several weeks to argue over how to handle her. Needless to say, Laurie failed to recover until her parents found a compromise. They spent a long time trying to work out a way of managing mealtimes that they both felt comfortable with. It meant they both had to change their behaviour but now they both approached the problem in the same way. As a consequence, Laurie knew that they were determined to try to work together to help her overcome her eating difficulties and gradually allowed herself to accept their help.

Jessie's parents were also unable to find a consistent approach to their thirteen-year-old daughter's anorexia nervosa. In their case, however, they were able to agree with each other on what to do but unable to adopt one particular approach for more than a day or two. Thus they would try one technique, for example offering rewards for a couple of days, but instead of staying with this for several weeks, they gave up after two days and then tried threats. Once they had adopted a consistent approach, day after day, Jessie started to improve.

Tom, fourteen, had always been a conscientious and diligent pupil. A year after his father died unexpectedly from a heart attack, Tom decided to go on a diet to protect himself from heart disease and he soon entered a downward spiral. His weight loss was so rapid that he needed urgent hospitalization, remaining in hospital for three months before he was well enough to return home. However, he then became very anxious about returning to school for fear of not being able to catch up with his work. His anxiety perpetuated his concerns about himself, his health and his abilities, with subsequent continuation of his eating difficulties. Once some additional tuition was organized he was able to cope with the planned return to school and began to recover.

Unfortunately, other perpetuating factors may be far less accessible to change.

Debbie was ten when her eating problems began. She had been ill for four years when she was referred to us, having lost half of her body weight. She was in a very distressed state. A particularly significant event appeared to have been the death of her grandfather when she was twelve. We discovered from an independent source that he had had previous convictions for sexually abusing children and it seemed likely that Debbie had been one of his victims. She acknowledged that something horrible had happened to her but was unable or unwilling to say more, indicating that if she did it would destroy her family. Debbie remained very ill and required long-term hospitalization.

In Debbie's case, although the apparent precipitating factor, sexual abuse, had ceased following her grandfather's death, her inability to allow herself to talk about it and get appropriate help was perpetuating the illness. It is only when perpetuating factors are remedied that the possibility of recovery can become a reality.

In summary, the causes of eating difficulties are numerous and almost always occur in combinations. No single factor can in itself be sufficient to create an eating disorder; rather, we need to consider the interaction between a range of factors, some of which are necessary preconditions for an eating disorder to develop (predisposing), others acting as triggers (precipitating) and yet others maintaining the problem once it has started (perpetuating). This is particularly important when deciding upon how best to manage the situation (see Chapters 4, 5 and 6). The flow-chart in Figure 1 summarizes our knowledge of the pathway by which eating disorders may develop.

Genetic factors operating via two pathways, biological and personality, combined with sociocultural pressure to be thin, render the child vulnerable to the development of anorexia nervosa or bulimia nervosa. On approaching or entering puberty, and with exposure to various stresses or traumas, the eating disorder emerges. Similar patterns, with less

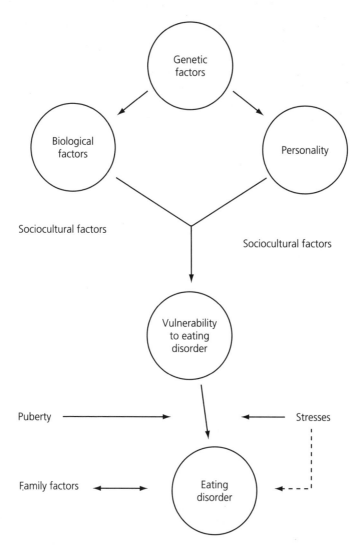

Figure 1 **The development of an eating disorder.**

influence by puberty or sociocultural factors, apply to other eating difficulties. Once the eating disorder has developed, those factors that may have contributed to it may still operate, e.g. sociocultural influences in anorexia nervosa, but other factors may then perpetuate it e.g. the sense of achievement or well-being from losing weight, or coercion to eat in selective eating or food phobia.

3

How do I know if my child has an eating disorder?

Nowadays, with all the publicity about eating disorders and the apparent increase in their incidence, many parents worry that their child has an eating disorder. As discussed in Chapter 1, there are many variations on 'normal eating', which although they may cause concern, are not really a problem. In this chapter we discuss what should alert parents to the possibility of an eating disorder and what they should look out for. We will try to provide some ideas about how to distinguish between normal variations in eating behaviour and changes that are more worrying. Clearly, there is a bit of a grey area between the two. Although sometimes it will be obvious that a child or a teenager has eating difficulties, this is not always the case. Often the problems are hidden or not acknowledged. Parents are frequently surprised by the extent to which their child has been able to hide changes in their feelings and behaviour.

The most obvious manifestation of an eating disorder is, of course, an alteration in eating patterns or a persisting unusual pattern. As mentioned in Chapter 1, there are a number of phases of childhood when eating commonly causes concern. In summary, these are the faddiness and the restrictive eating phases of the pre-school years, and the 'overeating' during the adolescent growth spurt. These are generally temporary phenomena and, as long as parents do not attempt to influence them too vigorously, they tend to resolve. It is difficult to put a time-line to these phases because there is considerable variation. In general, however, food faddiness during the pre-school years may last anything from a few weeks up to a year or two. As long as the child seems well, is growing and is happy, then there really is no cause for concern. Much the same can be said about the phase of restrictive eating during the pre-school years. In fact, this tends to have a shorter duration than food faddiness, rarely lasting for more than a few months. Again, if the child seems well, is growing and happy, then nothing needs to be done, and indeed it really is better to do nothing. Once undue anxiety and attention become attached to such patterns it is far more likely that they will persist and become the focus of tension and argument. If, however, the child is clearly unhappy, not growing as expected, or complaining of persistent pain, then it would be sensible to seek the advice of the doctor or health visitor.

The 'overeating' that can be so characteristic of adolescence is again, in most individuals, a normal phase, and in some ways one that is far easier to understand and accept than the toddler's or young child's restricted eating. Adolescence is a time of rapid growth and physical development, with the consequent need for a considerably increased calorie intake. In practice, this is manifested by the consumption of what may seem to be enormous amounts of food. Boys in particular may appear to be eating excessive amounts. There is really nothing unhealthy or abnormal about this. You need only worry if your child seems to be unhappy much of the time, expresses feelings of guilt around eating, is becoming overweight or if the overeating tends to be secretive and is accompanied by attempts to get rid of the food by vomiting or taking laxatives. The normal and healthy increased appetite of adolescence may persist for two or three years and, as long as the child is reasonably active, need not be a cause for concern but rather a source of pleasure that your child is thriving.

So what alterations in eating habits and other behaviour should cause concern? There are no hard-and-fast rules about this and what follow are guidelines. It is worth remembering that the whole of childhood and adolescence is a series of phases, some very short-lived, others longer, some persisting for a number of years. Therefore any change in eating may be a very transient phenomenon. In general, however, the longer such a change lasts the more likely it is to be problematic. This is all the more the case when the change in pattern is accompanied by other features such as secrecy, irritability, unhappiness, self-dislike or persistently illogical behaviour.

Anorexia nervosa and bulimia nervosa

We will start by describing the features of anorexia nervosa and bulimia nervosa, which have much in common (see Chapter 1). The onset of these eating disorders is often heralded by a child voluntarily going on a diet, often for no good reason. Even when she is not overweight she may insist that she is and that she needs to lose weight. Many children and teenagers who go on to develop eating disorders decide to become vegetarian, and some even vegan. They almost always account for this on moral grounds. Alternatively, you may notice that your daughter has reduced her food intake without making any comment about dieting. She has simply stopped eating as much as she used to and, when challenged about this, is likely to deny any problem, claiming she just doesn't feel particularly hungry.

As anorexia nervosa or bulimia nervosa develop, there tends to be an increased preoccupation with food, nutrition and calories, as well as a change in general behaviour. There is much overlap in behaviour between the two disorders, but there are also some differences. Much of the behaviour is secretive and therefore not necessarily obvious. The changes that indicate an eating disorder can be classified as:

- food-related
- general mood and behaviour
- physical.

We have summarized them in list form and where a behaviour or finding is specific to anorexia nervosa or bulimia nervosa, rather than both, we have marked it accordingly as AN or BN.

Food-related features
- preoccupation with food

- spending long periods of time reading cookery books
- sensitivity about eating
- very restricted eating (AN)
- preference for eating alone
- cooking meals for the family
- choosing low-calorie foods to the exclusion of anything else (AN)
- irritability, distress and arguing, especially around mealtimes and often over small quantities such as whether to eat five or ten peas (AN)
- strange behaviour around food, such as cutting or crumbling food into pieces, smearing it over the plate, or moving small pieces of food from one part of the plate to another (AN)
- hiding food under the plate or table, or in napkins or clothes pockets (AN)
- leaving the table during the meal, or immediately after, often to go to the bathroom
- collecting and storing food
- secretive eating
- bingeing (BN)
- vomiting (self-induced)
- denying hunger when it is obvious that she is hungry
- measuring self-worth in terms of weight or the amount of food eaten
- feeling distressed and guilty about eating
- inability to tolerate unplanned events involving food
- extreme irritability when meals are earlier or later than usual
- using a lot of salt, vinegar or spicy substances (AN)
- drinking a lot of water (often to make it easier to be sick)
- drinking a lot of diet cola or other low-calorie fizzy drinks (to help take away hunger pangs).

General behaviour
There are many other behavioural signs of an eating disorder, besides those related specifically to food, eating and mealtimes. These include:

- frequent weighing

- excessive exercising, especially before or after eating, e.g. walking everywhere, doing a large number of press-ups, repeatedly running up and down stairs, lane swimming
- increased willingness to do things involving exercise
- gathering information on dieting from leaflets, books and magazines
- using laxatives or so-called 'appetite-suppressant' pills
- using diuretics ('water pills')
- wearing baggy clothes (AN)
- having difficulty sleeping
- general irritability, especially when questioned about eating
- increase in activities unrelated to food, such as homework and sports (AN)
- increased interest in issues such as starvation in the developing countries (AN)
- increase in attempts to help others, e.g. doing voluntary work
- self-dislike
- defiance and stubbornness
- development of rigid daily routines
- social withdrawal and even isolation
- insisting she is fat when it is obvious that she is not overweight
- extreme fear of gaining weight
- other forms of self-harming, e.g. scratching, abusing drugs or alcohol.

Physical features
Weight loss, marked fluctuations in weight, purging activities (particularly vomiting and laxative abuse) and excessive exercising all have a number of physical consequences. The most evident of these are:

- weight loss, which can be quite extreme (AN)
- weight fluctuations, but generally around average weight (BN)
- loss of, or failure to start periods (AN)
- loss of, irregular, or failure to start periods (BN)
- dizziness, sometimes fainting

- tiredness
- stomach pains and feeling full when only small amounts of food have been eaten (AN)
- low body temperature with a marked tendency to feel the cold (AN)
- poor temperature control – either too hot or too cold (AN)
- poor blood circulation leading to cold hands and feet and, if untreated, to sores which don't heal, and can even become ulcerated (AN)
- skin on hands and feet has a purplish colour (AN)
- skin generally has a yellowish hue (can arise from eating excessive amounts of carrots) (AN)
- development of fine downy hair on the back (AN)
- loss of any pubic or underarm hair (AN)
- head hair becomes dull, lifeless and may fall out (AN)
- constipation (AN)
- mouth ulcers and tooth erosion
- swollen cheeks (enlargement of the parotid glands, i.e. those glands that also become swollen in mumps)
- calluses on the back of the fingers (due to rubbing against the teeth when inducing vomiting)
- tension headaches
- cramps in limbs
- polycystic ovaries (cysts on the ovaries diagnosed using ultrasound)
- thin bones (AN).

It can be seen that anorexia nervosa and bulimia nervosa can have serious physical consequences. A number of tests may need to be carried out; these are discussed in Chapter 6.

Children with other eating problems will have some features in common with anorexia nervosa when weight loss is a main feature, but there are some differences. We will discuss each in turn.

Selective eating

The most striking feature of this condition is the extremely narrow range of foods the child eats (see Chapter 1). The fact that a child may eat nothing but cheese, peanut-butter sand-wiches and ice cream, and drink only apple juice, for several years without coming to any harm is quite amazing. In a few cases, the child's diet may lead to a slight iron deficiency or a lower than recommended calcium or vitamin intake. However, we have seen many children on similarly selective diets without any obvious adverse physical effects. In particular, they seem to grow normally and not be unduly thin. They may, however, have dental problems, which is a particular problem in children whose diet includes a lot of sugary foods and drinks. Such children may suffer from frequent tooth-ache and need to see a dentist for treatment of dental caries.

The behaviour of children with selective eating tends to be otherwise normal, unless they feel forced into eating a wider range of foods than they feel comfortable with, in which case they are likely to become upset and demoralized. Some problems may arise around the age of eight or so when the selective eating makes it difficult for the child to go to parties or stay over with friends. It is usual for the range of foods gradually to increase during adolescence, as the pressure to conform to peer-group norms is quite strong.

Restrictive eating

The most striking feature is the limited amount (as opposed to range) of food eaten. Such children seem to manage on far fewer calories than most. Although they are often quite thin, they do seem otherwise relatively healthy and they rarely show the complications that are so common in anorexia ner-vosa. It is as if some children are just programmed to eat less than others, and they are also programmed to be thin. Indeed, there is often a family history of others having a similar pattern of food intake. There is little that parents can do that will make much difference, and fortunately this does not matter because these children seem to grow into perfectly healthy adults. The main things for parents of restricted eaters to keep an eye on are the child's growth, development and general mood and behaviour. If these seem to be adversely affected, or there are serious concerns, then it is sensible to seek further advice.

Tim had always been a poor eater. He fed well as a baby, but had never seemed particularly interested in food since being weaned. His mother had tried hard when he was a toddler to get him to eat what she thought were normal amounts, but Tim only ever ate a small portion of whatever she prepared. Tim's mother had been reassured that he was growing normally. On the health visitor's chart his height was always just below average and his weight rose steadily, staying in the same low-average range. Both the doctor and the health visitor had said there was nothing to be worried about. Tim was now eight and still ate only small amounts. At breakfast he would often just have a glass of milk and half a piece of toast. His mother wasn't sure what he ate at lunchtime at school but he usually said he'd had some of whatever was on the menu. He didn't come home saying he was starving, like his older sister did, but would eat a biscuit if he was offered one. At suppertime, Tim would have the same as the rest of the family but again he would never eat very much. Sometimes he skipped dessert, saying he'd had enough.

Tim's mother learned not to worry about his eating. He seemed well settled in school and had a number of friends. He was quite a quiet boy, not very sporty, but he had plenty of other interests. In many ways his eating was very like that of her husband. Tim's father was a slight man who also just didn't seem to have much of an appetite. His general health was good. When he was at work he often forgot to have lunch. He would eat three meals with the family at weekends and on holidays, but rarely ate snacks, although he would on special occasions. Tim's father enjoyed the food that he ate but he seemed simply not to need very much of it. It seemed that Tim was just like him in this respect.

Like children with selective eating, those with restricted eating show few other behavioural problems providing no pressure is applied to them around their eating habits. If, however, they feel forced to eat more, they are likely to become distressed and defiant. Generally, such children do seem rather more sensitive than most but not to the extent that other problems invariably arise.

Food phobia

These children often cause a great deal of concern because they can be extremely resistant to eating and drinking. As stated in Chapter 1, some of them have a fear of swallowing and may particularly avoid foods of a certain texture and sometimes taste. Such children usually indicate a fear of choking, gagging or being sick, or they may say that eating and drinking hurts. Other children may develop specific fears around certain foods, such as fear of being poisoned, which leads them to refuse a wide range of foods that they may previously have eaten without difficulty. Mealtimes are usually a battleground, with parents making desperate attempts to get their child to eat and the child in turn making just as desperate attempts to avoid eating, usually driven by extreme fear. Some children with this type of problem may manage on what they will eat, perhaps because the few foods and drinks they do take contain adequate calories and nutrients. However, others may lose a lot of weight and become very ill through a more comprehensive refusal to eat a normal diet. Parents will usually know if their child has a food phobia because the fear and anxiety around eating new or disliked foods is obvious. The following descriptions illustrate the sorts of problems children with food phobias present.

Lucy, twelve, developed a conviction that she must not eat chicken or anything with egg in it because it might be unsafe and make her violently sick. She had had a bad tummy bug with sickness and diarrhoea six months previously and had attributed this to a meal of chicken and chips at a local restaurant. At first, her mother was prepared to avoid serving chicken but when Lucy included eggs, and anything including any traces of egg, the whole thing became much more of a problem. Lucy refused to eat biscuits, cakes, some types of bread, and anything she knew or thought might contain egg. When she was unsure, because she had not been able to study a label, or when eating out, Lucy would become anxious. She would go pale and sweaty and often gagged on whatever she was eating. Her parents initially expressed their irritation and told her to stop being so silly, but became more worried as Lucy's problems began to get worse. By the time they took her to see the doctor, Lucy had been refusing to eat school dinners because she didn't know what was in them, and would only eat food prepared at home.

Adam, eleven, had feared eating and drinking since a particularly traumatic incident when he was eight. He was being investigated for poor appetite and feeling sick. He had a test that involved passing a tube into his stomach. He was very anxious and resisted the test. Unfortunately, the doctor persevered and Adam became completely panic-stricken. From that time on he found swallowing terrifying.

The physical consequences of food phobia depend on whether the child is of low weight or has a fairly rapid episode of weight loss. Food-phobic children who have a long-standing difficulty with eating may be both short and thin, depending on the length of time the problem has been in existence and the adequacy of their intake. This is probably because the body may have had years to adjust to a low-calorie intake, and compensates accordingly. In other children, who like Lucy develop a pronounced fear and avoidance of a wide range of foods, weight loss can be dramatic. As with anorexia nervosa, the body has to respond to fairly sudden starvation and does not have time to compensate before the complications arise.

Food avoidance emotional disorder (FAED)

The food avoidance in these children is but one aspect of their problem and, to this extent FAED is quite like anorexia nervosa. However, children with FAED tend not to be terrified of gaining weight, nor do they tend to be frightened of food or swallowing, nor do they have an aversion to taste or texture, so less fuss is made at mealtimes. Indeed, such children often wish they could eat more and are concerned about being thin. This is in considerable contrast to anorexia nervosa. The loss of appetite underlying the food avoidance seems to be genuine and is usually associated with depression, anxiety or obsessionality.

In children with FAED, there is a more generalized behavioural disturbance, which by no means centres on food and meals. Sadness and/or anxiety predominate and may pervade all aspects of the child's life. She is likely to be worried and miserable, with poor sleep and appetite, and have difficulty concentrating. She may have obsessional behaviour and is likely to avoid peer-group contact. More likely she will want to stay at home and may try to avoid going to school.

Compulsive overeating

This condition has more similarities to bulimia nervosa than any of the other conditions mentioned in this chapter, in that it is the only other one in which overeating persistently occurs. Unlike bulimia, however, the abnormal eating has usually been present for a long time and there is no disturbance in perception of body shape or size. Nor is there any concerted attempt to lose weight. The child may be unhappy about her size and appearance but make little effort to change it. In fact, her unhappiness with herself may lead her to eat more. Indeed, compulsive overeating is the only eating disturbance in which the child is overweight.

Food is often ravenously sought and can be eaten at any time of the day or night. Parental attempts to restrict intake are met with considerable resistance and, if dieting is imposed, secretive eating is used to compensate. It is not uncommon for such children to raid the fridge and even locked food cupboards. They may 'borrow' money so that they can buy snacks when out of the house, or even steal food at school or from shops. They do indeed seem to have a craving for food, particularly when unhappy or anxious. This creates a vicious circle, for compulsive overeaters are usually unhappy children, often with few friends, and possibly not doing well at school. They can become quite rebellious and stubborn and generally find life hard.

The physical complications are those associated with being overweight, and will depend upon the degree of excess weight. In the short term there are no serious complications. As time goes by, however, breathlessness on exertion occurs, and in extreme cases even at rest. In the long run, joint problems, diabetes and high blood pressure may occur.

In summary, there are a number of eating disturbances in childhood and adolescence, with quite different characteristics. We have tried to make a clear distinction between them but this is not always easy, as there is some overlap. In addition, most conditions have some variations, which can add to the confusion. However, we hope that this chapter has helped you to decide whether your child does indeed have some form of eating disorder or whether the eating pattern is simply a harmless phase or variation of normal behaviour. In the next chapter we discuss how to decide whether or not to seek professional help, who to go to and what they are likely to do.

4

What can I do? General principles

(*Note*: this chapter should be read in conjunction with
Chapters 5 and 6.)

Parenting is one of life's most difficult tasks and yet one for
which we receive very little preparation. Even when things
are going normally, parents may still wonder if they are
doing things right. For example, the temper tantrums and
food faddiness of the pre-school years, and the defiance and
rebelliousness of adolescence are normal and healthy
phases that tend to occur at different stages of development.
None the less, parents often feel mystified, worried and
challenged by them, even though these behaviours are very
common. It is hardly surprising then, that when a child
develops an eating disorder parents often feel at a loss as to
how to proceed. This is not at all unusual but hearing that
you are not alone in feeling at a loss is not much help.

In this chapter we offer some suggestions on how to manage your child's eating problem and some guidelines about
when to seek professional help. You will probably find it most
helpful to read this chapter in conjunction with Chapters 5
and 6. Regardless of the type of eating problem your child has,
do read through the sections entitled Crucial Principles and
Fundamental Points of Management before and after reading
the section relating to your child's particular problem.

If you are going to be in the best position to help your
child, it is our view that some crucial principles need to be
fully understood and accepted, and some fundamental points
of management implemented. These crucial principles and
fundamental points of management have come from many
years of working with children with eating disorders and
their families. It is our experience that when these guide-

lines are followed, the situation usually improves. So let us start with the crucial principles that need to be understood and accepted.

Crucial principles

1. No one *chooses* to have an eating disorder and no one particularly likes having one. Your child is no more choosing to have an eating problem than you might choose to have an ulcer or high blood pressure, which might be your body's response to a particular set of circumstances. These circumstances will be a combination of your biological make-up and what is going on in your life. We have seen in Chapter 2 that eating disorders seem to develop through the coming-together of a number of different factors. These are complicated multi-determined disorders that occur for complex reasons, almost invariably uninvited and unwanted. Often, however, a child can seem to be very attached to her eating disorder and it can be extremely frustrating for parents to meet what appears to be unbending stubbornness when they try to help. It is most likely that your child would give up her eating disorder, if only she knew how, despite behaviour that seems to contradict this, just as willingly as *you* would give up some other physical condition that you might suffer, if only you knew how. She does not know how, and she is often frightened by attempts to help her, as the eating disorder does seem to bring some advantages.

2. Resistance to change and resistance to help are integral parts of the condition, just as chest pain and shortness of breath are integral parts of a heart attack. The fact that your child resists help and may even deny that there is a problem does not mean she is being deliberately difficult. Rather, it reflects her fears; just as we might fear going to the dentist if we knew we were going to have a tooth extracted without an anaesthetic. It is important to remember that eating disorders develop as a response to a life situation that the child finds she can no longer manage using her usual coping strategies. The eating disorder usually serves a purpose; it has a function and represents some kind of a solution. Although it

is not a very healthy solution, it can be useful to think of it in this way, as it can help us go some way to understanding why it is so difficult, and often terrifying, for the child to give it up. This resistance to change, and resistance to accepting offers of help, is especially strong in anorexia nervosa (but, as we have mentioned, paradoxically success at being anorexic can seem to boost self-esteem).

3. In anorexia nervosa and bulimia nervosa, poor self-esteem is a crucial underlying issue. Although it may seem that your child is focused almost exclusively on food, calories, eating, weight and shape, underlying this is usually the fact that she has a really poor view of herself. She may see herself as a failure, not worth much or as a burden to her family. She may be deeply ashamed and feel that she is useless at everything. It can be hard to imagine that your child may be so dismissive about herself, particularly as (in many cases) she may well have been a previously popular and successful child. Again, what seems so obvious and clear to those of us on the outside cannot be seen by the child with the eating disorder. This is both frustrating and upsetting for parents. The poor self-esteem pervades the child's whole being and colours her view of herself and her life. She *genuinely* sees herself as a fat, unworthy failure and it can be very difficult to help her shift from this belief. (This unrealistic self-image is absolutely characteristic of anorexia nervosa and bulimia nervosa, but doesn't necessarily occur in the other eating problems.)

4. The worrying behaviours associated with eating disorders are likely to persist for several months, even after the problems have been correctly identified and appropriate steps taken to help overcome them. There is no easy route to overcoming them, no short-cut to success. Any expectation that there is going to be a rapid return to normal is bound to be disappointed. Far better to be prepared for a long, hard haul, for then frustration and disappointment are reduced.

If you are going to succeed in helping your child overcome her eating difficulties, you do need not only to understand these points but also to accept them and allow them to have an effect on the way you approach tackling the problem. If you take the view that your child is *choosing* to behave in this way, and that she could eat properly if she would only put her mind to it, then the chances of her recovering are negligible. However, if you can accept that what is happening is a reflection of a level of distress and not a reflection of how deliberately difficult your child can be, then you are on the right track and you can then begin to help her get better.

Just as there are some crucial principles, as outlined above, with regard to understanding the problem, so there are some fundamental points with regard to how to go about managing the problem. Successful implementation of these will in our view maximize the chances for your child's recovery. Later in the chapter we will describe specific methods of tackling the different eating problems. In this section, however, we need to emphasize these general, but fundamental, management points.

Fundamental points of management

1. Try not to blame your child for her eating problem. You are bound to feel worried, angry and exasperated at times; you wouldn't be human if you didn't, and you are very likely to express your frustration occasionally. Some parents will be inclined to do this more than others. The frustration is borne out of a complex mixture of emotions, with a combination of love for your child and feelings of helplessness as a parent usually being predominant. Expressing your feelings by venting your frustration doesn't make you a bad parent, just a normal one. However, your child is already likely to feel bad about herself, and about the fact that she is causing you so much distress. If you are persistently cross and short-tempered because of the impact the eating problems are having on you and the rest of the family, your child will tend to feel worse.

Becky's mother had been worried about her daughter's eating since the beginning of term. She didn't seem to be coming home from school complaining of being hungry, as she had done previously. Her mother noticed that she now always refused offers of something to eat or drink when they were out as a family. She became really worried when she went to a swimming gala at Becky's school and realized with a shock that her daughter had lost quite a bit of weight. Becky had been quite dismissive on the way home in the car and had gone upstairs as soon as they got home saying she had loads of homework. Her mother decided not to mention anything at supper time because her other daughter had a friend over and she did not want to embarrass Becky.

Later in the evening she told her husband about her concern. He had not noticed anything and said that she shouldn't worry too much; she had enough to cope with, with work and running the family. He thought that it was probably just a phase and that Becky would come out of it. If she was getting too thin then she could put some weight on. He suggested to his wife that if she was really worried she should take Becky to see the GP.

For Becky's mother, the situation seemed to go from bad to worse. She became very aware of how little Becky was eating but every time she tried to encourage her to eat more it ended in a huge row. She knew how much her husband hated arguments at mealtimes. He had a stressful job and worked long hours, and now that the children were a bit older they all ate together in the evening.

Becky's mother began to be very worried that her daughter may have an eating disorder. She found some information on the Internet that made her even more concerned. She talked more with her husband, who tried to help by telling Becky that she was worrying her mother and needed to put some weight on. Mealtimes were becoming a nightmare, with Becky and her father shouting at each other, her mother crying and Becky's older sister and younger brother pushing their plates away or asking to leave the table. Each evening seemed worse than the last.

Becky's father was utterly exasperated. His wife was lying awake worrying most nights. She looked drained and tired, and was tearful most evenings when the children had gone to bed. He hated to see her going through this. His older daughter and his son seemed to spend most of their time in their bedrooms or out with friends. Becky was being completely impossible, refusing to eat a proper meal, causing arguments and upsetting everyone. The atmosphere at home was dreadful. He found himself becoming more and more frustrated by the whole situation, he couldn't understand what was happening and it was becoming clear that he could do very little about it. In fact it was getting worse. At this point he realized that they really did have a problem on their hands and that they needed help to sort it out.

2. Try to be understanding and to accept that your child is in distress. She will usually feel badly about herself and what she is doing. Express your love and affection as much as you can. Explain to her that you are worried about her and that you do want to help, even though she may neither ask for help nor accept it when offered. None the less, like everyone else, she needs to know that she is loved and valued.

Zoe had been struggling with anorexia nervosa for a number of months. It had taken quite a while for her to be seen with her parents by someone who knew about eating disorders. The GP had done all she could in terms of offering support while they were waiting for the assessment appointment but it had been really difficult, with many arguments and tears.

Now that Zoe and her parents had been to the clinic a few times her parents were beginning to become more aware of what they could do to help. They had previously felt completely defeated by the problem and had pinned their hopes on the 'experts' sorting Zoe out. They now understood that becoming angry and frustrated and shouting at Zoe not to be so selfish was not helpful. They had been helped to understand that becoming angry and frustrated was normal, and they shouldn't try to prevent this, but the important thing was not to direct this at Zoe but at her eating disorder. So they knew that it was better to say something like, 'This anorexia makes me so angry because of what it is doing to you', rather than 'Stop being so selfish, don't you see what you are doing to yourself?' They had been able to accept the idea that Zoe was struggling herself, that she wasn't exactly having much fun and that she needed to know that they were there for her to help her fight the eating disorder, rather than fighting against her.

3. If you are a parent reading this book, the chances are that you will already have tried many different ways to help your child with her difficulties. Some of them may have helped a bit but probably none of them will have completely sorted out the problem. In the next chapter we will describe specific techniques that you can use for the different types of

eating problems. Here, however, we want to emphasize another critical point.

If a team is to be successful, the team members have to work together. In the same way, if parents are going to succeed in helping their child to recover, they too must work together. So what does this mean in practice? No technique can work unless both parents are using it consistently. You will need to maintain a united front through what is going to be a long hard haul. You will need to decide and agree a way of approaching the problem that feels comfortable to you both. It is possible and even likely that you will have found it hard to agree on a particular approach, and that you have used different methods. You may have to make compromises so that you can reach an agreement. It is also likely that you will have chopped and changed as time has gone by. Unfortunately this cannot work. Your child needs you to adopt an approach that you both use and that you stick with over time. The same point applies when other adults, such as grandparents, are involved. If you are a single parent it is likely that from time to time you get help from another adult, a friend or a grandparent perhaps. Assuming this to be the case then exactly the same principles apply.

Zoe's parents had at first tried to help her in their own different ways. Her mother could see how upset Zoe became at mealtimes and knew her daughter was unhappy. She found it very difficult to insist that Zoe ate what she was supposed to when there were so many tears. It made her feel as if she was being hard and cruel, and that it was she who was upsetting Zoe.

However, she knew that Zoe needed to eat more because she was becoming painfully thin. At first she had tried sitting down with Zoe to work out what she felt she could manage, and what might make mealtimes feel less stressful. She knew the plan that they came up with was not enough, and she knew that she was only serving up tiny portions, but at least Zoe did not cry so much. Her mother had hoped that if Zoe could be more relaxed at mealtimes she would gradually eat more.

Zoe's father had taken a different approach. He was extremely concerned about his daughter and the way forward seemed clear. He and his wife must insist that Zoe ate more for her own good. He felt they had no time to lose. When he saw how little was on Zoe's plate he often became angry. He would take Zoe's plate and put more food on it and would ask his wife how she ever thought Zoe would get better if she didn't feed her properly. This then led to a row between him and his wife, and, of course, to Zoe eating next to nothing.

Now that the family was attending the clinic, Zoe's parents had changed their approach. They had spent a long time together coming to an agreement about how to handle mealtimes. They were both exhausted by the arguments and were worried that Zoe did not seem to be getting any better and that their relationship was suffering. They both had to compromise, with Zoe's mother agreeing to try to be a little firmer and Zoe's father agreeing to try to be patient. They drew up a plan, which involved a gradual increase in amounts of food, which they told Zoe they would help her with. They promised not to change the plan or to go faster or slower, so that Zoe knew exactly what was expected of her.

Implementing the plan proved to be very hard. There were tears, Zoe's mother often found it difficult to stick to what was agreed and Zoe's father struggled to hold back. Both parents had tried to identify what would be the hardest times for them and they had agreed how they would help each other deal with these. Zoe's mother found that getting Zoe to eat her afternoon snack after school the hardest. She was usually tired herself at that time, still had a lot to do and had always enjoyed having a chat with Zoe about her day. Her parents had agreed that they would speak on the phone at this time, so that Zoe's father could remind her mother of why she had to insist and to support his wife in doing this by reminding her that they were working together. Zoe's father found the evening meal the most frustrating and relied on his wife's help to steer the topic of conversation away from food.

We are talking here about consistency – consistency between the adults looking after the child with the eating problem and consistency over time. It can take weeks for a particular method of tackling a problem to work, and this is assuming that it is being used by all the adults involved, all the time. This is such a fundamental point that it cannot be over-emphasized. Without consistency no child can make a sustained recovery from an eating problem. It is only when she has had the experience of her parents working together in harmony, and understanding and supporting her, that she can find the confidence to confront her fears.

Very slowly, Zoe got more used to the idea that her parents were determined to work together and stick to their plan. The tears and arguments were becoming less and she was slowly increasing her food intake. She felt anxious and afraid about this but was able to begin to talk about it, because she knew that her parents were trying to help. She also knew from the discussions they had at the clinic that her parents were not finding this at all easy, but were prepared to stick at it for her sake. Even though she still wished she didn't have to eat as much, and she still felt guilty after every meal, she found herself becoming more confused about what was happening and wanting to talk about it. It comforted her to know that her parents were clear about how to proceed and she knew that they would not spring any surprises on her.

4. Try not to lose sight of the healthy and good things about your child. Eating problems are often so worrying that it can become difficult to focus on anything else. Yet the more you can pay attention to the healthy side of your child, the more likely she is to recover. Sometimes this can be quite difficult to do, especially if your child is an adolescent. Normal adolescent development includes a process of challenging parental norms and values. This is a healthy and important stage in the process of developing autonomy, independence and a stronger sense of self. Adolescents need to experiment in all kinds of different ways as part of their development. This can at times be extremely trying, inconvenient and sometimes worrying, but just as adolescents need to work actively at the transition to adulthood, parents need to go through a process of adjusting the terms of their relationship to their child. Of course, parents have a responsibility to educate and guide their children so that they are less likely to place themselves at risk or harm themselves but a degree of 'letting go' is very important if young people are to flourish.

So some of the things your adolescent child wishes or chooses to do may not fit with your taste or way of thinking, but may be important in terms of normal development. Obviously, parents have a right to draw the line at some point but relatively harmless expressions of individuality should be encouraged. For example, the teenager's bedroom is a common source of dispute. Adolescents, like adults, need a private and personal space. The state and decor of this space may not coincide with your own taste or standards but basic rules of hygiene and consideration for others should be encouraged. The task for parents of adolescents is to allow *contained* opportunity for experimentation and individual expression, while maintaining certain boundaries in terms of social behaviour and personal responsibility. Not an easy task!

If you have an adolescent with an eating disorder, it is very important indeed to keep sight of the fact that a degree of rebelliousness and a challenging of your values is normal. This is a healthy side of your child, just as a continued interest in music or literature may be a healthy side of your child. The eating disorder already has a tendency to take over everything and put development on hold; as parents you will need to work hard at limiting its ability to interfere.

In the next chapter we will discuss when you should seek professional help. However, if you are in the slightest doubt do visit your doctor. Eating problems can be very difficult to overcome and can have serious complications. Don't avoid seeking help just because you think the reaction may be 'You are wasting my time'. Doctors are there to advise and reassure, as well as to diagnose and treat. It is part of their job to decide whether or not something really is a problem. If you are still in doubt, you can always take this book along with you to support your case!

Having discussed some crucial principles in the understanding of eating problems and some fundamental points in their management, we will now address the specifics for each of the eating disorders in turn. It is vital to remember that all the points we have just made apply regardless. They form the foundation of any treatment and without them, no specific techniques can work.

5

What can I do?
Specific problems

Anorexia nervosa

This is probably the most difficult and challenging of the eating disorders and understandably causes parents immense concern. You should certainly seek professional help (see Chapter 6) but you as parents are in a stronger position than anyone else to help your child to recover. When considering the suggestions outlined in this section do remember the crucial principles and fundamental management points made in the previous chapter. Don't hesitate to read them again and then, if necessary, re-read them.

You will need to discuss and use strategies for tackling such problems as abnormal or restricted eating, self-induced vomiting and excessive exercising. These are such common features of anorexia nervosa that you may be safest to assume that not only are they going to occur but that they will continue to occur for weeks or even months. It is better therefore to expect them rather than to be surprised by them. This can often be very difficult for parents. You may feel absolutely certain that your child would never make herself sick, hide or throw away food, or exercise excessively, but remember that she is quite desperate not to put on weight and that the anorexia nervosa will be making her behave in ways that are indeed unlike her. By expecting these behaviours as part of the problem you can then be prepared for them. So what strategies might you adopt?

As stated above, there are no absolutely correct methods of dealing with these behaviours other than having ways that both parents agree and feel comfortable with, and can apply consistently, both between each other and over time. What this will look like in detail will differ between families. It is important that you take responsibility for your child's health and safety, and therefore for her eating adequately. Usually people with anorexia nervosa try to take command of the family's eating, even to the extent of wanting to buy and cook the food. We have found that it is not helpful to let this happen, but rather that parents should take responsibility for buying, cooking and presenting the food, as well as trying to ensure that enough is eaten. We advise that this be the family rule. So long as your child is allowed to take over meal arrangements she is unlikely to get better.

Mia was thirteen years old and had anorexia nervosa. She had always been a very capable, competent, sensible and reliable girl. She lived with her mother and stepfather, younger brother and seventeen-year-old stepsister Ginny. Mia would only eat food that she had bought with her mother. Each Saturday morning she and her mother went to the supermarket and Mia put the things she would eat in the trolley. She usually got exactly the same things, including a number of low-calorie ready-made meals and some fat-free yoghurts. She carefully read the labels of new things to check for calorie content and fat content but mostly she stuck with the packets and brands she knew. Her mother usually bought other things for the rest of the family. Mia tended to eat different things from them at mealtimes and her mother had learned that it was easier to allow Mia to choose exactly what she wanted, otherwise there were tremendous tantrums and rows and she refused to eat anything at all.

Mia's mother did not think it was right to buy so many ready-made meals and had explained to Mia many times that it was just too expensive. Sometimes she tried to make something for Mia herself but it always ended up with Mia standing in the kitchen watching her like a hawk and telling her how to do it. If Mia hadn't seen her mother prepare the meal she would refuse to eat it. This was becoming a real problem between Mia's mother and Ginny. Ginny thought her stepmother was being utterly useless and that Mia was just a spoilt child. One Sunday there was a row between Mia and her mother about whether you had to use butter to make a white sauce, which Mia won. The whole family then sat down to a meal with a watery sauce, which Ginny said was completely disgusting and couldn't everyone see how Mia was ruling the whole family. She then left the table and stormed out of the house. At this point, it was clear that Mia's insistence on controlling the shopping and cooking could not continue.

Once it is accepted that you are taking responsibility for meals, you will need to agree how to help your child to eat. Your options range from taking a very coercive approach at one extreme, to letting her eat what she wants, over whatever period of time she needs, at the other. It is unlikely that either extreme will be beneficial and you will need to find your own middle ground.

Decisions that you will need to make include: how much she should try to eat at any one sitting; how long the sitting should last; where the meal should be eaten; who should be there and where they should sit; who should provide encouragement and support, and how. You may well wish to take your child's wishes about all of this into consideration but you should not be ruled by her. You will need to use your own judgement as to what is sensible, remembering that her judgement is impaired, that she is truly desperate to avoid eating and that she will use every means she can to avoid doing so. In summary, you will need to have a plan that deals with each of the issues raised in this paragraph.

Darren's parents had found it helpful to draw up a weekly plan for mealtimes, which they looked at each evening with Darren (see Table 1). Darren's chart looked slightly different each week, partly because different things happened each week, and partly because it was part of the plan that he would gradually add a bit to the amount that he was eating, and would try to get through meals a bit quicker. This particular week, he had been invited back to his friend James's house for tea on Tuesday, his parents were due to go to the theatre on Friday evening and his grandparents and aunt were coming for Sunday lunch. Darren's parents discussed with him the sort of things and amount he would need to eat at teatime at James's. They helped him rehearse what he could do if he wasn't offered a snack. Darren practiced saying 'I'm really hungry, can we ask your Mum if we can have something to eat?' This was an occasion where Darren was given

Table 1 Darren's mealtime plan

Time	Length of meal	Where meal is eaten	Who is present	Who is in charge?
MONDAY				
Breakfast	15 min	Kitchen	Mum and Dad	Mum and Dad
Snack	15 min	Teacher's room	Teacher	Teacher
Lunch	30 min	School cafeteria	Friends	Teacher
Tea	15 min	Kitchen	Mum	Mum
Supper	45 min	Kitchen	Mum and Dad	Mum and Dad
TUESDAY				
Breakfast	15 min	Kitchen	Mum and Dad	Mum and Dad
Snack	15 min	Teacher's room	Teacher	Teacher
Lunch	30 min	School cafeteria	Friends	Teacher
Tea	15 min	James' house	James and James' Mum	Darren
Supper	45 min	James' house	James and James' Mum	Darren
WEDNESDAY				
Breakfast	15 min	Kitchen	Mum and Dad	Mum and Dad
Snack	15 min	Teacher's room	Teacher	Teacher
Lunch	30 min	School cafeteria	Friends	Teacher
Tea	15 min	Kitchen	Mum	Mum
Supper	45 min	Kitchen	Mum and Dad	Mum and Dad
THURSDAY				
Breakfast	15 min	Kitchen	Mum and Dad	Mum and Dad
Snack	15 min	Teacher's room	Teacher	Teacher
Lunch	30 min	School cafeteria	Friends	Teacher
Tea	15 min	Kitchen	Mum	Mum
Supper	45 min	Kitchen	Mum and Dad	Mum and Dad

Table 1 cont.

Time	Length of meal	Where meal is eaten	Who is present	Who is in charge?
FRIDAY				
Breakfast	15 min	Kitchen	Mum and Dad	Mum and Dad
Snack	15 min	Teacher's room	Teacher	Teacher
Lunch	30 min	School cafeteria	Friends	Teacher
Tea	15 min	Kitchen	Sally	Sally
Supper	45 min	Kitchen	Sally	Sally
SATURDAY				
Breakfast	15 min	Kitchen	Mum and Dad	Mum and Dad
Snack	15 min	Kitchen	Mum and Dad	Mum and Dad
Lunch	30 min	Kitchen	Mum and Dad	Mum and Dad
Tea	15 min	Kitchen	Mum and Dad	Mum and Dad
Supper	45 min	Kitchen	Mum and Dad	Mum and Dad
SUNDAY				
Breakfast	15 min	Kitchen	Dad	Dad
Snack	15 min	Kitchen	Mum and Dad	Mum and Dad
Lunch	1 h	Dining room	Mum, Dad, Aunt and Grandparents	Dad
Tea	nil			
Supper	30 min	Kitchen	Mum and Dad	Mum and Dad

responsibility for sticking to the plan himself. For all the other meal-times it was clear who would help him; sometimes it was Mum and Dad, sometimes just one of them. On Friday evening it would be Sally the babysitter, who Darren got on well with, and on Sunday at lunch-time, which Darren was dreading, his Dad would keep an eye on things.

When Darren's parents had been working out how to help him, they had made an appointment to see Darren's teacher and the head teacher of his school to discuss his problems. His teacher had noticed that he had lost some weight and had been concerned about this, but she reported that his academic work did not seem to be suffering in the least. She had observed that he seemed to be a bit more withdrawn and was not playing with the other children so much. Together they discussed a plan that would allow Darren to have supervised mealtimes but that would hopefully minimize any embar-rassment and separation from his classmates. At morning breaktime, the rest of the school did not usually have a snack. There was a water fountain in the playground, but that was all. Darren's parents agreed with the teacher and head teacher that at morning break he would go to Mrs Paul's room for his snack. Mrs Paul was the art teacher, and while he was having his milk and biscuit Darren sat and helped her sort out the pots of pencils and felt-tips, sharpening the crayons, and doing other odd jobs. He was free to go as soon as he had finished his snack and when his friends asked him why he always went to Mrs Paul's in morning break he knew to reply that he was working on a special project; it was pretty boring but it should be over soon. This was after all true. It had been agreed that as soon as Darren's weight became less of a worry, morning snack during school time could be dropped. With Mrs Paul's and the school's help Darren was therefore able to have what he needed, while being supervised, but in a way that did not make him lose face with his peers. At lunchtimes he sat with his classmates because it did not seem right to isolate him. At his school the children had a choice between a hot meal, a cold meal or a jacket potato with filling. Darren's teacher gave him the following week's menu each Friday so that he would know what he should be asking for each day. Darren's mother sent the menu back on Monday mornings with Darren's choices for the week ringed. His teacher then took responsibility for ensuring that the member of staff on lunchtime duty kept an eye on Darren and that he was eating what he was supposed to. In this way, again, he was supervised but in a way that would not cause him embarrassment in front of his peers.

Using the weekly chart really did seem to help Darren move forward with his eating. He was able to reduce the time it took him to finish his meals and he usually managed to stick to the amounts he was supposed to have. It also helped his parents as they shared the responsibility for supervising, and giving encouragement and support. Darren's mother looked forward to Sunday mornings when she had breakfast in bed while her husband had breakfast downstairs with Darren. Darren's father made a real effort to get home from work at a reasonable time so as to be there at suppertime, and he and Darren had some time together just before bedtime, when Darren had his last snack.

In the acute stages of the illness, eating patterns and habits can be very disturbed. The main thing is to make sure that your child eats enough. Our view is that it doesn't matter so much what she eats, where she eats, when she eats, or who is present. The crucial point here is that your child resumes eating adequately. A dietitian or your family doctor can advise on calorie and nutritional requirements. These are different for different stages of growth and development. Whatever is done to ensure that your child does eat adequately is good enough at this stage. You can worry about the other aspects later (see below). At this stage, she must eat enough to stop losing weight and to survive and, as the weeks go by and she gets used to eating more, enough to put on weight and to thrive.

Adele's parents were really struggling to get her to eat anything other than tiny amounts of food. They knew that they had to do something about this because she was continuing to lose weight and was becoming quite weak. At their last visit to the clinic they had been advised to think about an admission because of Adele's deteriorating physical health. They knew how much Adele was supposed to be eating but knew it was so much more than she was ever able to manage that they felt very pessimistic about their ability to help her have what she needed. It had been suggested to them that they might try some fortified drinks. This had not occurred to them before. Adele's mother thought that they were the sort of milky drinks that you gave to elderly people with weak digestions. However, she went to the chemist and found a brand of drink powder that came in different flavours, which you could drink like a milk shake. The drink was very high in calories and had added vitamins and minerals; it was, as the carton said, 'a meal in itself'.

After lengthy discussion, Adele finally agreed to try it. It was the school holidays and her parents had already had a long discussion with her about how to stay out of hospital. Adele chose the strawberry flavour and agreed to have a small glassful after each meal, and at three snacktimes. She continued to eat only tiny amounts from her plate but was able to drink the strawberry milk down. Her parents had suggested to her that she should think of it like medicine, that it wasn't something she wanted to or necessarily chose to have, but had to. After a while, Adele complained of being sick of the strawberry flavour, and she tried a few of the other flavours instead.

Through drinking the fortified drink Adele was in fact getting many more of the calories and nutrients she needed and her physical state slowly began to improve. She managed to stay out of hospital but her parents still had a lot of hard work to do in helping her to tolerate increased amounts of food.

Most people with anorexia nervosa not only use obvious ways to avoid eating or to cut out high-calorie foods, but also use hidden means. It is common to hide food in napkins, under the table, or in pockets. Trips to the bathroom occur far more often than is necessary, especially during and immediately after meals; excessive exercising is also common among people with anorexia nervosa. You will need strategies to deal with each of these. For example, you might encourage your child to go to the bathroom before a meal, but not during a meal or for two hours afterwards. It is unrealistic to expect a child to be able to give up exercising completely; in any event a certain amount of exercise is healthy. Therefore you should decide on how much you allow and how much you dissuade.

Kate had gradually increased her level of exercise, and was spending more and more of her day trying to burn off calories. When she woke in the morning she did exercises secretly in her room. If she had time she then took the dog out for a walk before she went to school. The walk was more of a run and her mother often commented on how exhausted the dog seemed. At home she always ran up the stairs two at a time, and seemed to be forever running up and down. She seemed unable to sit still and often went out on her bicycle for hours on end. At school she had signed up for a lot of after-school sporting activities, which she had never really been interested in before, and she became upset and angry when for some reason she couldn't go.

Kate's parents had read that exercising was often a problem that accompanied an eating disorder, which they knew Kate had, and even though they were not aware of at least half of what Kate did by way of exercise, they decided that they needed to try to help her limit it. They set aside time to try to talk to Kate about it all. She was very against the idea of taking less exercise as she felt that that would make things even harder for her. She was trying to stick to what she saw as a ridiculous diet, which was going to make her fat, and wondered how they could expect her to do more. It would be completely unbearable to have to eat huge meals and then not be allowed to take any exercise. It took a long time to reach the situation where her parents decided together that they would not allow her to push herself to the limit any longer. They agreed between themselves that they would not allow the long bicycle rides and the after-school squash sessions, but that Kate could continue with her swimming and that she would be allowed to take the dog for a walk. It was not easy to put this plan into practice but they knew that it was the right thing to do, and they had made it clear to Kate that she could increase her level of exercise as soon as she was able to demonstrate to them that she could take responsibility for eating enough.

Be prepared for considerable resistance and conflict; it is going to occur. Try to see this as part of the eating disorder and realize that it is likely to last for some time. In this way you protect yourself from too much disappointment. Through the inevitable battles do try to remember also that your child is in the grip of something she has not chosen to have and that she is not deliberately setting out to be awkward. It really helps her if you can keep sight of her positive aspects and the fact that she needs reassurance that you still love and value her.

Pippa felt utterly miserable. She worried constantly about what she had eaten and dreaded each meal. She felt she couldn't continue to make the huge effort she had been making and that no one really had any idea how difficult it was for her to get through every single mouthful. Before meals she felt anxious and tense and irritable and after meals she felt fat and disgusting and panicky. She always seemed to be snapping at her mother or shouting and arguing. She felt very bad about this because she knew that none of this was her mother's fault. She couldn't help it though, because her mother was always there, ready to push more food down her throat.

Pippa's mother was beginning to understand what was happening. At first she couldn't understand it at all; Pippa had never been so rude and inconsiderate. They had come through a lot together, since Pippa's father had left them three years previously. Pippa had been a great support and good company, and her mother was very distressed by what was now happening to their relationship. She could see how ill Pippa was and was determined to do what she could to restore her daughter's physical health. Even though she had been told to expect fights and arguments, nothing could prepare her for the scenes that took place on a daily basis at mealtimes.

Pippa's mother knew that Pippa was very frightened of putting on weight. It was hard to believe this because it seemed so obvious that Pippa was extremely underweight. She often screamed at her mother, 'Why do you want to make me fat?' with such loathing that it was clear that Pippa really was frightened and really did see herself as ugly and unlovable. Her mother had found it very useful to be able to talk things over with her own sister. She knew that her task was to be strong and solid. She had to insist that Pippa ate at mealtimes, even though that meant she got a barrage of abuse and hateful looks. She had learnt to manage this by reminding herself that the hatred and abuse were for the eating disorder not for her, and that she was not fighting with Pippa but with the eating disorder. The stronger Pippa's reaction, the more determined her mother was to overcome this dreadful thing that was taking over Pippa's life and personality.

Pippa herself felt exhausted and ashamed. She had to protest because she knew it was wrong to eat. It really helped her that every now and then her mother would come and give her a big hug, even though Pippa had been shouting and screaming at her and once broke her mother's favourite vase by throwing her plate across the room. Pippa's mother came and gave her a hug and said that they had got through difficult times before together, and would get through this. She reminded Pippa of how they had coped together before, and of her strengths, which had allowed her to do this. Pippa knew her mother loved her and was there for her, despite her behaviour.

We have found it helpful to remind parents that the child with anorexia nervosa is experiencing two conflicting internal messages or 'voices'. The first voice is telling her that she is fat, bad and ugly and that she shouldn't eat, and the second – usually a smaller, quieter voice – is saying that she is ill, thin and should eat. The first voice is experienced by everyone as being much louder and stronger than the second, and it is very easy to get caught up in conversation and argument with it. Sometimes children give a name or an imagined form to this anorectic voice, and describe it as being present for most of their waking hours. Our preference is to talk to the healthy voice along the following lines:

'I know how strong the "voice" is that tells you you are fat and shouldn't eat; how much at times it torments you, but at other times seems to be your friend. It must be very confusing and frightening for you. But I want to speak to the healthy part of you, the non-anorectic part of you, so I am not going to speak with the anorectic part.'

We find that refusing to get into arguments with the 'anorectic voice' avoids unnecessary confrontations. In any event, that voice represents the illness and all its lack of logic, and is not open to reason, so there is little point in trying to reason with it. It is far more useful to encourage the healthy part by talking to that part rather than to the unhealthy part.

Lisa imagined her anorexia nervosa as a green scaly creature with a large beak that was always with her. It always knew how much she ate and always scolded her after mealtimes for eating too much. It made her promise to try to cut down and told her she should always be on the move. It reminded her that to be fat and ugly was to be a useless, worthless, unlovable human being, and that she needed to work hard to avoid this. Other people were trying to make her fat and she had to stop them.

Lisa had started to see a therapist as she had become so ill. She had told her therapist about the green scaly creature, and had said that sometimes she didn't like having it around, but that she had got used to it, and at least it kept her on the right track. The therapist had said that she had been hoping to have some conversations with Lisa, not the scaly creature, and that she would be a bit fed up if the scaly creature kept sticking its beak in.

During one session, Lisa drew a picture of the creature, which she coloured in. The therapist then suggested that each time Lisa came to see her, they would put the picture of the creature in an envelope and put it in the bottom drawer of the desk so that she and Lisa could talk in peace. This worked well in allowing Lisa's 'healthy side' to talk. Sometimes, when her anorectic thinking crept into the conversation, the therapist would say, 'Can you hear who I can hear?' and they would put the envelope deep in the filing cabinet, or even in the room next door. They were then able to discuss the things it was most difficult for the creature to hear without interrupting.

Lisa took the picture home after each session and gradually began to use it in the way that she did in her sessions. She put the picture upstairs before she came down to meals, and her parents helped her to be aware of when it was interrupting. Eventually, after many months, Lisa was only very occasionally bothered by the creature. She knew now that it talked rubbish.

Until now we have been focusing on how to manage mealtimes and the urge to get rid of or burn-up calories. Away from the meal table, it is important also to focus on the underlying feelings. Your child is likely to be feeling frightened, miserable, guilty, bad about herself, angry and confused, yet she is unlikely to be able to talk about it. She needs to have these feelings acknowledged and accepted. Unless this is done, she will remain unable to talk about them, and is likely to remain demoralized by them. A useful statement would be something like:

'I think I can imagine how awful you feel; I do love you and I wish there was something I could do to help.'

She may respond with an unspoken sign that she does want to be comforted, in which case a warm hug cannot do any harm. At the other extreme she may yell something like:

'You don't understand. You are stupid and I hate you. Why don't you just leave me alone.'

Our advice would be to say something along the lines of:

'OK, perhaps I don't understand, but I still love you and I am going to do everything I can to help you.'

It is helpful to be aware of the advantages your child perceives in maintaining a low weight. As outlined in Chapter 2, most people with anorexia nervosa feel very good about losing weight. They have a sense of pride, reassurance, control and achievement, all of which contribute to the feeling of well-being, and they feel desperate at the thought that they might lose all this by putting on weight. It is not useful to challenge this as it only leads to conflict and withdrawal. Rather, you should encourage her to talk about these feelings and acknowledge how good she feels about herself. In doing this she is then more likely to listen to you.

Your child needs this sort of reassurance to help her cope with all her inner turmoil, as well as needing to know that you do indeed care and have the strength to help her fight the battle against the anorexia nervosa.

In summary:

- remember the crucial principles and the fundamental points
- remember that people with anorexia nervosa experience many benefits to having it
- take a firm stance around ensuring her health and safety
- have a strategy to deal with the food avoidance and related behaviours
- ensure consistency between adults and over time
- talk with the 'healthy voice' rather than the 'anorectic voice'
- offer repeated love and reassurance.

These approaches are very likely to lead to a gradual improvement. Be patient and be prepared to persevere. The illness will take a long time to disappear but if you give up, or change your approach, it will take even longer.

As your child begins to start eating again, she is very likely to enter a stage of extreme anger, defiance and rebellion. If she has not already done so, she will begin to express very powerful and bitter feelings to those around her. We

have now seen this so often that we have even given the process a name; we call it 'stage two'. This is to acknowledge
that it follows the first stage of anorexia nervosa – the
characteristic problems with eating and the distorted and
negative view of self (see Figure 2).

   Stage two usually starts about four to eight weeks after
people with anorexia nervosa start eating again, although
there can be considerable variation in timing. Eating
remains problematic and it seems as if the situation has
actually got worse, especially as stage two can last for up to
several months and is a very trying time indeed for parents.
The one good thing that can be said about it is that its onset
does herald recovery. If you can tolerate it and do not
attempt to suppress it, then your child's eating and mood
will gradually improve and she then stands a very good
chance of making a complete recovery. If, in contrast, you try
to block stage two, you will almost certainly succeed and
your daughter will revert to her determined food avoidance
and related problems. It is as if your child must go right
through this stage to make a complete recovery. This is

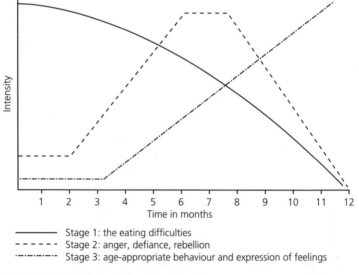

Figure 2 **Stages of anorexia nervosa.**

probably because she needs to pour out all these feelings, however unjustified they might seem to you and others around her.

It is worth repeating that to most people there does not appear to be much logic to this disorder, and seeking it adds to the frustration and despair. We don't look for the logic of a malignant disease in which the body cells start destroying the body. We don't start arguing with it but we do get on and attempt to treat it. So, with anorexia nervosa, there is no point in trying to convince your daughter that she is behaving unreasonably. She cannot help it. Rather we get on with treatment.

You will need to decide how much stage two behaviour you can allow. We usually advise parents to tolerate as much as they can but to set limits. In other words, you will probably need to allow the anger outbursts and the insults, however painful these may be. You can encourage physical outlets for these feelings, such as punching a pillow or kicking a beanbag. However, you would probably not allow physical aggression or damage. These rules and limits need to be absolutely clear, and consistently enforced. In this way your child will feel safe to express her painful feelings in the knowledge that you would not allow them to get totally out of control.

Melanie had entered stage two. She shouted, slammed doors, threw things and generally banged and stamped around the house not caring who or what was in her way. Melanie's parents had just about had enough. They had been forewarned that Melanie would be likely to become more assertive and expressive as she began to eat and put on weight. They had also been advised that when this happened they might seriously consider pulling Melanie out of treatment because it might seem as if she was worse. It was a good thing they knew that this dreadful phase meant that Melanie was on the road to recovery because what was happening seemed completely out of character and quite unacceptable. What made matters worse was that they knew very well that Melanie was perfectly well behaved at school and was fine when she was out with other people.

Melanie's parents got to the stage where they had to sit down with Melanie and draw up some limits to her behaviour. They understood that she needed to express her anger and frustration but there had to be some boundaries. They decided that Melanie would be allowed to shout at them but that she should not swear in front of her younger brother. If she felt she needed to swear, she could go to the shed at the bottom of the garden and shout and swear and scream all she wanted. She should not throw china or glass, but could throw soft objects in the playroom. If she needed to kick a door, she should kick the garage or the shed door. If she broke or damaged anything she would have to pay to replace it.

They had a difficult period of a few weeks when Melanie seemed about to burst with anger and irritation. They let themselves be called all kinds of names and be accused of being the most unloving, uncaring parents that had ever existed. Gradually, though, through their ability to withstand what Melanie was throwing at them and through their insistence that she should stick to the rules that they had drawn up, the difficult behaviour began to lessen.

If you can manage to follow these guidelines then your daughter is likely to move into stage three, in which she begins to eat more normally, develop a more realistic view of herself and express her feelings, including difficult or negative feelings, more appropriately. There is overlap between all three stages (see Figure 2) and this can be confusing. However, our experience is that children who go through all of these stages are very likely to make a full and sustained recovery. Your child should be no different providing you follow all the guidelines in this chapter.

Bulimia nervosa

The management of bulimia nervosa has both similarities to and differences from anorexia nervosa. You should certainly re-read Chapter 4 in which we outline the crucial principles in understanding the eating disorders and the fundamental points in their management. As with anorexia nervosa, your child will not have chosen to develop bulimia but might be more willing to try to have a go at getting over it. In general, people with bulimia nervosa are more able to recognize that they have a problem than those with anorexia nervosa, and this is obviously a very necessary step in the right direction in trying to tackle the problem. You will, however, still encounter resistance to change because the bulimia often serves a function, just as the anorexia can. Your child will be being encouraged to give up something that she has developed as a response to a difficult-to-manage situation. It will not be easy for her to do this without addressing other things as well. As with anorexia nervosa, this can be a lengthy process.

Low self-esteem, and its underlying issues, is also very much a feature of bulimia nervosa. Indeed, many of the thoughts and behaviours characteristic of anorexia nervosa are also found in bulimia. For this reason, it may be helpful to read the sections on anorexia nervosa. There are, however, some important differences (see Chapter 3). For example, in anorexia nervosa there may be either food avoidance alone or the eating of small amounts followed by purging, leading to low weight. In contrast, in bulimia nervosa, food avoidance, if it occurs, is punctuated by episodes of overeating. Eating patterns are irregular and often chaotic. The most striking feature is the tendency to binge then purge (usually achieved through self-induced vomiting or using laxatives) or starve, leading to the maintenance of relatively normal weight.

If your child has, or you suspect her to have, bulimia nervosa, it would be wise to seek professional advice (see Chapter 6) because bulimia nervosa can have major medical complications (see Chapter 3). Furthermore, certain medications have been shown to help reduce the urge to binge, which your doctor may feel would be appropriate.

Your management as parents needs to focus on helping to regularize eating, avoid purging and other weight-control behaviours, and improve self-esteem. You will not have the same worries about weight loss that parents of children with anorexia nervosa experience. On the other hand, repeated vomiting and laxative abuse can be very dangerous and do need to be controlled.

In contrast to someone with anorexia nervosa, you may find that your child is more able to admit her difficulties and may even want help. However, you need not be too surprised if this is not always the case, as there may be variation from day to day, as well as from person to person.

There is no need to try to take control of your child's eating habits; in fact this would probably be counterproductive. Rather, try to enter into teamwork with her. It may well be useful to ask her what help she wants to get things back under control. You shouldn't expect her to be able to stop bingeing and vomiting immediately; this is far more likely to be a gradual process. It can be helpful to plan strategies for implementing a gradual reduction of these episodes, for example trying to reduce the number of binges from seven to six a week, and then to five. It helps to find distractions to use when the urge to binge arises. For example, when the urge does occur, perhaps you could all agree that she tells you, rather than giving in and secretly bingeing. You could then help her to resist the urge either by 'talking her through it' or offering other distractions. These may seem quite artificial but are worth trying. You can all use your creativity to work out what would be a useful distraction; going for a walk or run, watching a video, telephoning a friend, are examples. Whatever strategies you use, remember that change will be gradual.

Milly was in the process of struggling to overcome her bulimia nervosa. It had taken her a long time to be able to begin to talk with her mother about her problem. She was very ashamed and embarrassed, but knew she had to tell her because her mother knew that food kept disappearing. Her parents had had no idea that she made herself sick every night while they were there, and she had not yet been able to talk to them about being sick at school after lunch. A further problem was that Milly had run out of money to buy the food she needed for binges. She had often bought a large amount of food on her way home from school, secretly eaten it and been sick in the toilets in the park. She had on occasion stolen money out of her mother's purse, which she felt was a dreadful thing to do.

Milly agreed that her mother should talk to her father. She herself was too ashamed to do so. Both her parents were upset that she had not talked to them sooner. They arranged to seek advice and were now trying to help Milly get her eating under control. They agreed to start by trying to cut down on the bingeing and being sick in the evenings. They drew up a list of things that Milly could do after supper, when it was hardest for her. At first, her parents suggested things like reading a book or watching television, but Milly said she couldn't concentrate on that kind of thing. In the end, they agreed on a list which included going for a walk on the downs with her mother or father, going for a bicycle ride with either of her parents, or going for a drive with her father, with loud rock music playing on the car stereo (which her mother hated!).

At first, there were many walks and bicycle rides in the dark but Milly found that she could manage not to make herself sick on an increasing number of nights. It was hard for her, and she really had to work at resisting the urge. She found that the presence of her parents, and the ways they tried to distract her, helped a lot. She would never be sick in front of them. Once Milly had managed to reduce her evening bingeing and vomiting she felt she had achieved something, but she knew she still had a very long way to go to stop being sick after lunch at school. The next stage would be to sit down and work out a plan to help her resist the urge when her parents were not around.

As in anorexia nervosa, poor self-esteem and difficulty in coping with painful feelings are crucial underlying issues in bulimia nervosa, which need to be addressed. Indeed, many people with bulimia nervosa report that the urge to binge often occurs when they are feeling sad, worried or angry.

Sita had good days and bad days with her eating. On bad days she made herself sick two or three times. She didn't wake up in the morning knowing what kind of day it would be, but often something would happen that would turn it into a bad day. Sita was a rather shy girl. She did not think that she was very pretty and felt that she was not as clever or as funny as the other girls in her class. She was quiet and hardworking and she wished she had more friends at school. She mostly spent time with her cousins and family at the weekends and almost never met up with her classmates outside school. She somehow felt different and that she just did not fit in.

Sita gradually began to recognize the sorts of things that made her binge. These included making mistakes in her work, being with girls in her class who were laughing and joking about things she didn't understand or know anything about, accidentally making people cross with her, and being the last to be chosen during the sports lesson. When these things happened, she felt even more useless and unhappy. She recognized that when she felt like this, she usually binged then needed to clear herself out by making herself sick.

It may be helpful to try to discuss the way in which bingeing occurs in response to distress, so that alternative means of coping can be considered and tried. This will usually involve helping your child to express her distress more directly, by talking, becoming angry, crying, rather than trying to cope with the difficult feelings by bingeing and vomiting.

There are now a number of self-help manuals available, which are well worth trying (see the Further Reading list). Although these have not been written specifically for children and adolescents, it may be worth you getting hold of a copy and reading one because the self-help manuals might well help you to help your child tackle her bulimia.

Selective eating

While you are very likely to be anxious about your child's narrow range of foods, it is unlikely that any real harm is being done (see Chapter 3). This can often be hard to believe, because everyone now knows about the importance of a properly balanced diet. It may seem that as your child is only accepting a few foods, she can't possibly be getting what she needs. However, the diets of most selective eaters, although restricted to only a few types of food and drink, will in fact contain sufficient amounts of protein, carbohydrates, fat, vitamins and minerals to sustain healthy growth. In consequence there really is little that you need to do at all, particularly if your child is not upset or worried about her eating.

The one exception is selective eaters whose diet has a very high sugar content or whose preferred drink is a fizzy sweet one. Such children tend to experience considerable dental problems and you should ensure that you arrange regular visits to the dentist. An added complication here is that selective eaters are often very reluctant to see a dentist. This is presumably related to the fact that these children tend to be particularly sensitive to things being put in their mouths. They are very resistant to new tastes and textures of food, and many find the experience of visiting the dentist extremely aversive. It is worth persisting with trying to reduce this anxiety to avoid the long-term consequences of neglected tooth decay. It is very likely that your child will grow out of her selective eating patterns, but she has to stay with the same set of teeth for the rest of her life. The vast majority of selective eaters do grow out of their restricted acceptance of different foods. In many cases, we have not found treatment to be particularly helpful in the short term. Although intensive treatment may have some slight effect, it is often limited, and it can sometimes have the opposite effect of emphasizing the child's difference from others. It can also make food and mealtimes a battleground. We have found it far more useful to try to accept the narrow diet, in the expectation that it will change in time, after ensuring that no harm is being done in terms of physical growth and development.

Lola was eight years old and due to change schools later in the year. She first came to the clinic after the Easter holidays, when she had one term left at her first school. Lola felt comfortable at school. She had been there since she was four, she knew all the teachers and she had always been able to take her packed lunch in with her. Everybody at school knew that Lola did not eat the cooked school dinners and no one made a fuss about it. While the other children had whatever the lunch was for that day, Lola always had her same lunch of plain chicken sandwiches, a packet of ready-salted crisps and two jam-sandwich biscuits. She drank water from the water fountain like the others. Sometimes Lola went to play with her friends after school and most of their mothers knew that she usually refused offers of tea or snacks, saying she would have something later at home.

Lola's parents had been putting off trying to do anything about her eating. However, with the change of school coming up they felt they had to try to get her to accept more different foods. The new school had a very clear rule that all children were expected to eat the meals provided. They offered a limited choice and no one brought in packed lunches. Lola herself was worried about this. She was also worried about going home with new friends, as their mothers might expect her to eat things that she did not like. During the Easter holidays her parents had made some disastrous attempts to get Lola to try some new things. It seemed clear they were getting nowhere, which prompted them to seek advice.

During the next term they worked at encouraging Lola to try some new things. They did this is two main ways. The first was that Lola's mother made the packed lunch very slightly different each day. Some days Lola had a different flavour or make of crisps. Some days she had different bread for her sandwiches, and sometimes she had a different filling. If Lola couldn't eat what was in her box she was to leave it, but she should be able to show her mother that she had at least tried. Lola was able to experiment at her own pace, without anyone else being particularly aware or making a fuss. By the end of term she was able to eat ham, chicken or chicken-paste sandwiches, three different flavours of crisps, a range of different biscuits, and she had introduced bananas and cheese triangles.

The second way they tried to help was to make use of Lola's wish to fit in with the other children in her new school. Instead of getting Lola's new uniform just before she started school, they got most of it together a few months early. At suppertime Lola would change into her new school uniform to come to the table. Her parents talked with her about how much more grown up she seemed, and helped her practise trying tiny amounts of new foods. Often she only had a spoonful, but at least she seemed more prepared to try. They helped Lola keep a record of all the new foods she had tried and what she thought about them. She thought most of them were disgusting, but some were 'not too bad' and one or two could be 'OK'.

The week before she was due to start school Lola's parents were feeling rather despondent. It felt as if they had been working on this for months, but had not come very far at all. Lola was still only eating a very restricted range of foods and they knew she would be faced with things at school that would be new to her. However, they underestimated how things seemed to Lola. She felt she had made a lot of progress and she knew that she could at least try new things. Her list of 'OK' things to eat was growing all the time.

Lola came with her parents to the clinic after a six-week gap. She had been at the new school for half a term and had settled in really well. She loved her new teacher, and had made friends. She seemed happy and settled. During the session she was eager to talk about the project she was doing and a planned visit to a Roman villa. When the conversation was steered around to school lunches, she reported that they were fine. For the first week she had been a bit wary and hadn't eaten too much, but it didn't seem to bother her too much now. She said that some days there was something revolting on the menu but there was usually something else she could have. She seemed very pleased that she wasn't the only one who thought some things were horrible. Lola's parents confirmed that things had improved dramatically. She seemed to have taken to the school lunches far better than they had expected. They puzzled about how slow the progress had been up until then, and knew that although Lola ate a wider variety at home than she had done in the past, it was nothing like the variety she ate at school. However, they agreed that it did not seem worth worrying about, Lola was happy and well, and the transition to the new school and new friendships had all gone smoothly.

One of the main concerns about selective eating relates to social situations such as parties, sleepovers and school trips. Many selective eaters prefer to evade such events to avoid the embarrassment of being different and the hunger of not eating. You can help your child in such circumstances by having an advance word with the adults who will be responsible. Most parents and teachers will be willing to accommodate the problem, once it has been carefully explained.

Max, aged ten, was very anxious because his godfather had invited him to come and stay for the weekend on his own, without his parents or younger brother and sister. Max liked his godfather very much and was keen to go. What made it better than anything was that his godfather had arranged for them to go to the television studios to be in the audience for the filming of Max's favourite programme. Max was a great television fan and to him nothing could be more exciting.

It had all been fine until his mother had asked him what he would do at mealtimes. Max was extremely fussy about his food, to the extent that he had to use a particular plate and cutlery as well as only having certain foods. He managed without the plate at school because he took a packed lunch. His mother reminded him that if he was going to stay for the whole weekend he would not be able just to take a packed lunch and he would have to eat at his godfather's house. He wanted to go, but knew he couldn't eat strange food.

In the end, he agreed that one of his parents could ring his godfather to explain about his eating. His father rang and explained about the plate and the cutlery and that Max would only eat certain foods. His godfather was quite surprised but very understanding. He suggested that Max and he should go shopping at the start of the weekend, to be sure to have a few of the right things around.

Often you will find that the less fuss is made the better. If you do feel you need to do something, because the eating difficulties are upsetting your child or otherwise interfering, then it may be helpful to seek further professional advice. However, you can discuss with your child what foods she might be prepared to try. You should not attempt to introduce more than one new food every few days, and this should only be offered in very small quantities, a teaspoonful or so. A very small reward could be also offered for any success, however small. Coercion, in contrast, can only be counter-productive. Remember that your child's natural response to peer-group involvement is to try to be as similar as possible, and that this usually leads to gradual resolution of the problem, especially in the early teens.

Restrictive eating

This is another condition that causes understandable concern to parents. Certainly you should seek a medical opinion but more often than not there is nothing to account for the restricted amount of food eaten. Encouragement, persuasion, coercion or force seem to make no difference, and are best avoided. So long as the medical opinion is that no harm is being done then it is best to leave well alone. If you feel compelled to do something then the techniques described above in the section on selective eating can be attempted. Remember, however, that giving too much attention to the problem, especially when coercion is used, is likely to make it worse.

Charlotte was nine years old and had a bird-like appetite. She was a small, petite child but had always been like this. Her younger brother was now taller than she was, even though Charlotte was two years older. He was a much more solid child and ate what his parents considered to be normal amounts, which was far more than Charlotte. Charlotte's mother had always been worried about her daughter's eating. She had struggled when Charlotte was a small child to get her to eat anything very much at all. She simply did not seem to be very hungry. What little she did eat represented a balanced diet – it just didn't seem enough. Charlotte's mother had often taken her to see the GP. They had a record of her growth, which showed her growing fairly constantly just above the third centile. The GP had tried to reassure her and had referred Charlotte to the paediatrician just to make sure. The paediatrician had also said there was no need for concern. Charlotte was growing and developing normally, and was eating enough to allow her to do so. She did not seem unduly tired or lethargic and appeared to be a normal child in all other respects who was in good general health.

Charlotte's mother had to listen to the comments of both her mother and her mother-in-law, who frequently told her that Charlotte needed 'feeding up'. They had no shortage of advice and suggestions as to what she should do.

Charlotte's mother hated these conversations as they increased her level of anxiety about Charlotte and made her feel that she was a useless mother. Even though the GP and the paediatrician had told her there was nothing to worry about, she did worry, and she felt a pressure to do something about it.

Charlotte's mother decided to make a real effort to insist that Charlotte ate more. She served up normal-sized portions and stood over Charlotte, making her eat every last mouthful. Charlotte complained of being full and not wanting to finish, but her mother insisted. After a few days of this the atmosphere in the house was awful. Charlotte was often tearful and upset; she became silent and withdrawn, and did not understand what was happening.

After a particularly awful Sunday lunchtime, Charlotte went for a walk with her father. Her mother was distressed and exhausted. Charlotte's father was alarmed at what seemed to be happening. He didn't agree with forcing Charlotte to eat more, but understood why his wife felt she had to do it. He was worried by what was happening to everyone. His wife was permanently irritable or tearful and last week they had had a note home from school asking if they were aware of anything that might be upsetting Charlotte, as she had 'not been herself' at school. They seemed to have gone from a situation where everything was more or less stable to one where Charlotte could not face mealtimes and was unable to concentrate at school, and his wife seemed to be falling to pieces. They needed to talk things over because if they continued like this, things could only go from bad to worse.

Food phobia

This is a condition that can be difficult to treat and which understandably causes much concern. It is advisable to seek professional help or support. As with restrictive and selective eating, coercion is counter-productive and tact, patience and perseverance are necessary. The techniques worth trying are very similar to those for restrictive and selective eating. In addition, the person you consult will probably recommend using a relaxation technique (see Chapter 6) and possibly some medication.

Fiona had a food phobia that took the form of a fear of swallowing 'bugs' with her food. She had learned about germs and bacteria and worried that, when she ate, her food would have 'bugs' on it that would multiply in her stomach and make her ill. She had distressing images and sometimes dreamt about this happening. Fiona managed her phobia by trying to eat things out of packets, which she had opened or seen being opened. Despite her parents' repeated reassurance and their continually pointing out that they did not become ill all the time, Fiona remained extremely food phobic.

Fiona's parents were trying to work with her to help reduce her anxiety levels at mealtimes. They tried to help her in a number of different ways. They tried to make sure they talked about neutral subjects at the table and that the topics of conversation were things that were of interest to Fiona. Her mother had bought her a little china cup into which she poured some 'special water' before each meal. They imagined that this water would help deal with any 'bugs' that might sneak in. They also got some books out of the library about how the body works and about how the body fights off illness and infection. Fiona began to understand that a healthy body is more able to do this than an unhealthy one.

Food avoidance emotional disorder

The main thing to remember with this condition is that the food avoidance is usually a consequence of some distress of a more generalized nature. In this respect it is like anorexia nervosa, but there is not the same terror of gaining weight nor misjudgement of body size. However, children with food avoidance emotional disorder will genuinely find it difficult to eat and, as with all the other types of eating problem discussed so far, coercion does not work.

Children with food avoidance emotional disorder (FAED) can often become extremely ill. They may lose a lot of weight and can be suffering from relatively severe emotional problems. Again, it is advisable to seek advice as your child may have both physical and psychological needs that will require attention. In any event, the underlying distress needs to be understood and hopefully resolved. This necessitates the same sort of patient exploration as we have described in the management of anorexia nervosa and bulimia nervosa. The weight loss with FAED may not be as worrying as in anorexia nervosa, and so there may be no need to tackle it as urgently. However, if there is considerable weight loss then the same principles of management apply.

Isobel, thirteen, was very thin and pale when she first came to the clinic. She had been off school for a while and was causing everyone a great deal of concern. Her GP thought that she probably had anorexia nervosa and referred her to the eating-disorders clinic. During the assessment it became clear that Isobel did not in fact have anorexia nervosa, but FAED. She knew that she was thin and that she needed to put on weight, but did not have the motivation or incentive to do so. She appeared anxious and was not particularly talkative and it was difficult to know what might have contributed to her current difficulties.

One thing was clear, however, and that was that Isobel was extremely underweight. She needed to regain some of the weight she had lost as a matter of some urgency. Isobel's parents were advised to try to adopt the fundamental points for management: to try not to blame Isobel for the situation; to try to be understanding and supportive, even though there was at this stage no obvious or clear reason why Isobel should be like this; to try to support each other as parents and to use firm encouragement to help her to eat more; and to continue to remember how Isobel had been before she became ill, and focus on her strengths and interests. This seemed very hard to do at first, because there did not seem to be a logical explanation for what had happened. However, they knew that Isobel was struggling with something that she did not yet seem ready or able to put into words. In the meantime, they accepted their main task as being the attempt to help her restore her physical health.

Compulsive overeating

This condition has most in common with bulimia nervosa, in that food intake is excessive and self-esteem is often low. The main difference is that purging, by using laxatives or self-induced vomiting, is absent. The critical principles and crucial points of management mentioned earlier in Chapter 4 are very relevant. If you can apply these then there is far more chance of influencing the situation for the good. As with bulimia nervosa, you are attempting to reduce food intake, encourage expression of feeling and different ways of coping with difficult feelings, and improve self-esteem. It is worth reading the section on the management of bulimia nervosa because many of the things you might try are similar.

We have now had a look at some of the things you as parents can do to help your child. Let's recap on some of the important points. In Chapter 4, we focused on crucial principles and fundamental points of management. These were as follows:

Crucial principles
- No one chooses to develop an eating disorder.
- Resistance to change and resistance to accepting help go hand in hand with the eating disorder, particularly in anorexia nervosa.
- Poor self-esteem is a core feature, particularly of anorexia nervosa and bulimia nervosa.

- Recovery, or getting 'on top' of the eating difficulty is likely to be a lengthy process.

Fundamental points of management
- Try not to blame.
- Try to be understanding and accepting.
- Try to be consistent as parents, working together if there are two of you.
- Try not to forget the healthy side of your child.
- Don't put off, or allow yourself to be put off, seeking help.

We have given a number of ideas and illustrations of how these points and principles can be translated into practice in the context of a range of types of eating problem. However, as we have seen, one of the fundamental points to remember is not to put off seeking help. As parents there may be only so far you can go on your own to help your child overcome her problems. This leads us into our next chapter, where we discuss who you can consult and what sort of help you might expect to receive.

Who should I consult and what will they do?

(*Note*: this chapter should be read in conjunction with Chapters 4 and 5.)

We have emphasized the importance of seeking professional help if you are worried about your child's eating or weight. Many of us worry about 'bothering the doctor' because he or she always seems so busy. However, we should not allow such concerns to get in the way of asking for help, advice or reassurance. Your child's health and happiness, rather than your doctor's busy schedule, should be your top priority.

Healthcare systems vary from one country to another so it is difficult to make general statements about who you should consult. However, most countries have general medical practitioners or family doctors, and in most cases this should be the person to consult first. In some countries (for example in the USA) it is more customary to go direct to a paediatrician.

Not all general practitioners or paediatricians will have a special knowledge of, or expertise in, eating disorders. Indeed, some may be rather surprised by the idea that children can have eating disorders like anorexia nervosa and bulimia nervosa, although with all the publicity over the last few years this should not be news to most doctors. Your own doctor may or may not be immediately responsive to your concerns. Sometimes you may be advised that your child is just going through an awkward stage that she will grow out of. What you need to do is give the doctor as clear a picture of the problem as you possibly can. It may help to say straight away that you are worried about your child's eating. If it has always been a problem then say so but if it is a relatively recent development then try to make this clear. For example, you could say that she was fine until about six months ago when she said she was going to be a vegetarian. This didn't bother you too much at first but you became really concerned when you saw how little she was eating and that she seems to have lost weight. You should point out other changes such as refusing to eat with others, moodiness, withdrawal, secretiveness, or irritability. If you feel she has an eating disorder then you should say so and explain why you believe she has.

The doctor should ask a number of questions, the aim of which will be to elicit more details of your concerns, your child's behaviour and her general health. You will usually have your child with you and the doctor will probably then ask questions of your child and seek agreement to examine her. Such an examination would probably include checking her weight and height, and her pulse and blood pressure. In the early stages of weight loss the pulse rate increases, but once the weight loss is marked the pulse rate slows and the blood pressure falls, leading to weakness, tiredness and dizzy spells, especially when standing up. The doctor may also listen to her chest, feel her abdomen, and check her skin colour and elasticity. The doctor might also check your child's back for lanugo hair and sores on the skin covering the bony parts of the spine and hips, and her feet for poor circulation and sores.

Such an examination should give a fairly clear impression of your child's general physical state. However, it is likely that the doctor will carry out some tests. Most commonly these will be blood tests but a urine specimen may be checked for infections and it is possible that some other investigations will be suggested, such as X-rays. The blood tests can show whether there is any anaemia, change in the white cells that fight off infection, or alteration in blood chemicals, all of which can occur with eating disorders. The results of these tests won't influence the diagnosis but can help with management.

Whatever tests are done, the doctor should make a preliminary statement about what might be wrong and what should be done. Clearly this will depend upon a number of factors. As already mentioned, some doctors attribute a change in eating patterns to being 'just a phase', saying your child will 'grow out of it'. This is sometimes true for preschool children but only rarely so for the older ones. If your doctor says this and you are not convinced then you should say so and explain why. For example, if your daughter says she is too fat when clearly she is thin, it is far more likely that she has an eating disorder requiring treatment than that it's just a phase. Sometimes the doctor may say that many youngsters go through a phase of dieting, thinking they are fat when they are not, and that it really isn't a worry. If this is the case, you can always point out that 'normal' dieting in children and adolescents is rarely long-lived and even more rarely leads to sustained weight loss. It may sometimes be necessary for you to be persistent and you will need to be prepared for this, but it is certainly worthwhile if you are genuinely concerned. However, for every doctor who may appear rather dismissive of your concerns, there are many more who will listen and take the appropriate steps outlined above.

Few doctors feel completely competent in the assessment and management of eating disorders and few will have the time or resources to offer much more than initial early intervention. Sometimes this may be sufficient but in many cases a referral will be suggested to some form of specialist or clinic. The choice of specialist will vary but might include a dietitian, paediatrician, child psychologist, child psychiatrist, nurse, social worker, counsellor, psychotherapist or family therapist.

Your doctor may recommend seeing a dietitian, who can advise on what constitutes an adequate daily intake for your child and how this might be composed. This may have value in some circumstances but is unlikely to be helpful as a sole treatment for an eating disorder. What is needed is an approach that addresses the underlying problems just as much as the inadequate food intake. In addition, you are going to need advice, support and counselling on how best to help as a parent. You can always ask the doctor what other help is available and what you should do if your daughter continues to refuse adequate nutrition despite a dietitian's advice.

If a dietitian is to be involved, do insist on going to the appointment yourself. Many, if not most, young people with eating disorders completely overestimate their food intake and therefore give a very misleading impression to the dietitian. Furthermore, they are likely to misrepresent what advice the dietitian has given. Most dietitians would see the parent as well as the child, but in case this does not seem to be the plan, do be prepared to insist on being present.

A paediatrician will be able to make a detailed assessment of your child's physical state and advise about any further investigations that need to be conducted. These might include more blood tests or X-rays or similar tests. The paediatrician may be looking at hormone levels and evaluating the state of growth and health of the bones. When nutrition is inadequate the bones may stop growing and may lose their density. It is particularly important to be aware of this because of the increased risk of osteoporosis in young people with eating disorders. It is also possible to check the state of the ovaries and uterus using ultrasound examination. In eating disorders these organs are commonly adversely affected, particularly in that they regress in their development. Visualizing them through ultrasound assists in determining the severity of the problem and helps in the monitoring of recovery.

The paediatrician may make a number of recommendations, such as referral to a dietitian (see above), vitamin supplements, high-calorie feeds or even, if particularly concerned, hospitalization. It is unlikely that the paediatrician will offer any treatment for the underlying aspects of the eating disorder, but rather will recommend referral to a specialist who can deal with the psychological issues.

The type of specialist who might see your child will differ from one clinic to another, and is often determined by who is available. There is considerable overlap in training and expertise between the different professional specialities. Clinical child psychologists are trained in both adult and child psychology and place a particular emphasis upon understanding and managing problems within a psychological and social framework. Child psychiatrists are medically qualified (and therefore may conduct physical examinations and investigations and prescribe medication) and have completed training in both adult and child psychiatry. As doctors they may place an emphasis on a medical model of understanding problems. Nurses, likewise, are usually trained within a medical model, but may have specialized in offering particular types of therapy or treatment. Social workers are primarily concerned with psychological and social issues. Counsellors and psychotherapists usually see people alone to help them understand and overcome their problems. Family therapists are trained specifically in helping families.

If there is any choice, you should ask for referral to a clinic that has a special interest in eating disorders. If there isn't such a clinic available then at least ask for referral to someone who has some expertise in eating disorders. It matters less whether they are a psychologist, psychiatrist, counsellor, psychotherapist, or family therapist, and more that they know how to deal with the different types of eating disorders, and that they know how to communicate with children. In particular, they should ensure that you remain centrally involved in the management. Be very wary of any approach that excludes you, because however skilled the specialist, you are still going to have to help your child at each meal for some time to come. Overcoming eating disorders can take weeks, months or even years. You need and deserve advice and support throughout this stressful time. Indeed, we believe that parental involvement in treatment is the single most essential aspect of the process.

It is also important to know that the different types of eating disturbance need different types of management. For example, if a child has anorexia nervosa then she needs quite different management to someone who suffers from bulimia nervosa or selective eating. Food phobia requires a quite different approach to food avoidance emotional disorder or restrictive eating, and so on. Indeed, each of the different types of eating problem requires its own specific treatment. Do not be afraid to ask about this, for you want to ensure that your child gets the right treatment.

What follows is an outline of what we believe should be offered for each of the different eating disorders. It reflects what we consider to be good practice and what we hope you and your child will be offered.

Again, the first and most important component of any treatment programme is your continuing involvement. Referral to a specialist should lead to a comprehensive (i.e. physical, psychological and social) assessment. Once this is complete the specialist should make a clear statement to you about the diagnosis, additional investigations needed, the course of the disorder, the likely outcome and what might be necessary by way of treatment. If this does not happen, ask for elaboration or clarification. Do not be satisfied with anything less.

Anorexia nervosa

The crucial aspects of management have already been outlined. There are two main strands to our approach. The first is to make clear that we are there to help and support parents in the task of helping their child; we are not there to take over. The second main focus is on trying to help parents to join with their child in fighting the anorexia. All too often the battle has become one between parents and child, as if she is being deliberately difficult and has actively and willingly chosen to starve herself. We emphasize that the eating disorder has a life of its own and has taken over their child. Usually we ask the young person with anorexia nervosa if any small part of her knows that she is ill and, if so, how much of her knows. A common conversation between one of us and the person with anorexia nervosa may go something like this:

'I have talked to a number of people of your age with this problem. Most of them have been able to tell me that there is a small part of them that recognizes that they are ill, although a much larger part of them can't see it that way. I wonder if there is a small part of you that can see that you are unwell, even if it's only a very small part, perhaps only about 5 per cent of you.'

Most youngsters are able to acknowledge that at times a part of them can see that they are ill. We would then ask them to try to tell us how big that part is. Again it is usually possible to get some estimate, such as 5 or 10 or 20 per cent. We then say that this is their healthy part, their real self, and that is the part of them we want to help and to get to know. We ask if the unhealthy part, which tells them they are fat and shouldn't eat has a name such as 'the anorexia' or 'the voice'. Sometimes they have given it a name; at other times they like the idea of giving it such a name (see Chapters 4 and 5).

This is a most important part of the treatment process because it establishes that the anorexia nervosa has an identity separate from the young person, and so allows us all to join together in our fight against it. This is not as far-fetched as it may sound. Although there isn't actually an audible voice, most people with anorexia nervosa are tormented by intrusive thoughts that they are fat. It is as if they are continuously hearing a voice, and our referring to the 'anorexic voice' acknowledges this. It also allows everyone involved to begin to distinguish between the healthy and unhealthy parts of the young person with anorexia nervosa.

Emma, fourteen, and her parents had been open to the idea that Emma's 'anorexic voice' was a real nuisance and that it was making life very difficult for Emma. At home, they tried to use some of the ideas they had talked about in their last session. Emma had described that she felt split in two about her eating. There was a part of her which very much wanted to be able to eat normally, to enjoy the things she had previously enjoyed, and not to have to worry all the time about her weight. There was another part of her which overshadowed this, which told her that she was greedy, that she needed to get a tighter hold on things and that she shouldn't trust anyone because they all just wanted to make her fat. During their last session, the therapist had suggested that this was the 'anorexic voice', which needed to be put in its place and clearly told to stop bothering Emma.

The following week, at mealtimes, her parents reminded her that the 'anorexic voice' would try to interfere, but that she knew they were there to help her make it go away. They encouraged Emma to tell them if it was very loud and they developed a number of different ways of trying to deal with it. Instead of getting angry with

Emma for refusing to eat what was on her plate, they got angry with the 'voice' for making it so hard for her.

We encourage parents to avoid arguments with the 'anorexic voice' for a number of reasons. Anorexia nervosa is a destructive and malicious illness. It does not have any obvious reason to it and therefore its voice is not open to sensible discussion. Furthermore, the voice appears to thrive on attention and argument. The more parents plead or argue with it the more it seems to thrive. When the voice is continuously ignored, the healthy person seems to re-emerge.

Jeanne, fifteen, had been unwell with anorexia nervosa for about nine months and had lost about 10 kg. She was eating very little and had become secretive and irritable. During the assessment at our clinic the following conversation was held:

Clinician to parents: 'Jeanne's anorexia has certainly got the better of her at present and it is important for you both to help her overcome it. This means that you are going to have to take charge of her eating for a while.'

Jeanne: 'Don't take any notice of him – he doesn't know what he is talking about and he doesn't care.'

Mother: 'Jeanne, you mustn't be rude to the . . .'

Jeanne: 'I don't care, he's stupid and I hate him.'

Father: 'How can you hate him? You don't even know him.'

Jeanne: 'He just wants to make me eat so I'll get even fatter.'

Clinician: 'This is an example of the anorexic voice speaking rather than the real Jeanne; it's best to ignore the anorexic voice and only talk to . . .'

Jeanne: 'He's really stupid – there isn't any voice and he doesn't know what he's talking about.'

Mother: 'Jeanne, just try and listen to what the doctor is saying.'

Clinician to parents: 'The best thing you can do at the moment to help Jeanne is not to talk to the anorexia; just ignore it completely. If the real Jeanne joins us that's fine and we should listen to her.'

Jeanne: 'How can you take any notice of him?'

Father: 'He is a specialist and has seen lots of girls like you with . . .'

Clinician: 'That is the anorexia still talking; try to ignore it.'

Jeanne: 'I am not going to eat, whatever he says . . .'

Mother to father: 'I think the doctor is right; we are always having these arguments and they don't get us anywhere.'

Jeanne: 'Daddy, please don't listen to them; they don't understand. They want to make me fat.'

Father: 'Jeanne, I will talk to you but not your anorexia.'

Jeanne: 'You all hate me. None of you care.'

Clinician: 'I don't know whether that was the real Jeanne or the anorexia; sometimes people do think that they are so awful that everyone hates them. Can one of you find out?'

Jeanne (in a much quieter and sadder voice): 'It is me.'

Mother: 'Do you really think we all hate you? Surely you know we love you. We've always loved you – we always will.'

Jeanne (still in a soft voice): 'Sometimes you seem to care more about Deborah and Tim [brother and sister].'

This discussion continued for several minutes before the 'anorexic voice' returned and trapped Jeanne's parents in a further fruitless argument. However, gradually they learned to ignore the voice and the real Jeanne became more vocal and talked about the things that had been upsetting her.

This approach helps parents to avoid the continuous, upsetting and useless arguments with which they have become so familiar.

As outlined in Chapters 4 and 5, it is essential that parents take responsibility for their child's health and safety. We work at helping parents find ways of ensuring this. For example, it is vital that parents are consistent in their approach to the problems, both consistent with each other and consistent over time. It is quite common for parents to have found this difficult. We ask each parent to outline how they want to tackle the problem and what help they want from the other parent. Given that there are likely to be considerable differences between parents, we then ask them to see if they can find some common ground. We don't make very specific suggestions ourselves for in so doing we are quite likely to propose something with which one or other parent feels uncomfortable or unable to do. It is far more useful for parents to find a way of working on the problem with which they both feel comfortable.

Steven's parents came to the clinic after a lengthy period of trying to find help for his eating disorder. Their experience had been that it was very difficult for people to accept that a thirteen-year-old boy could have anorexia nervosa, let alone be in a position to offer any constructive help. By the time they came to the clinic Steven had had numerous examinations and investigations and they and he had been seen by a large number of people. Throughout all of this, Steven had been losing weight and his parents' anxiety had been increasing. They were exhausted and frustrated, but very relieved because they believed that Steven was now in safe hands.

They were initially unsure when they were told that we were not there to take over and when they did not receive reassurance that we would get Steven well. It was explained to them that our role was to work with them, to help them get Steven back on the road to recovery. Their experience had been that Steven had such a difficult problem that not one of the whole string of professionals who had seen him so far had been able to deal with, so how could they be expected to sort it out?

We started by discussing what they felt might be a good way to try to help Steven increase his food intake. Both parents outlined a very different type of approach. When we asked what they had tried until now, they said that they thought they had tried everything, but that nothing worked and they had completely run out of new ideas. They had been hoping that we would have some.

On further discussion it transpired that they had actually been very creative in coming up with a lot of different ideas, but that Steven's father had tried to use some while his mother had tried to use others. Because of the differences in their style of handling problems they had effectively been cancelling out any positive benefit from the use of any one strategy. They could begin to see this and asked which approach we would recommend. We did not suggest any one idea, as this would have represented siding with the mother against the father, or vice versa. We explained that the point was that they should discuss and agree upon one approach and then stick to it, and that this process was more important than the details of what they decided to do.

After a lot of discussion and compromise they developed a plan that they both felt reasonably comfortable with. This plan contained many things they thought they had tried before and they were very sceptical that it would do any good. However, they were reminded that the main difference this time was that they would both be doing the same things, and that they had both made a commitment to sticking to the plan, even if it didn't seem to have any immediate effect. They agreed to give it a go.

As illustrated in Steven's situation, we emphasize the importance of sticking with a particular approach for at least a couple of weeks and probably longer. We often find that parents try a particular approach for a day or two and then abandon it because it hasn't worked. Unfortunately, any approach will need some weeks before it truly shows benefit.

Steven's parents put their plan into practice between sessions. For the first two weeks it seemed they were making little or no progress. Mealtimes remained horrendous and they both had moments when they thought that what they were doing was pointless and would never make Steven better. They had agreed, however, to stick to the plan for the two weeks between the sessions, whatever happened, and then to come back and discuss where they had got up to.

At the next session they appeared demoralized, tired and fed up. Steven's father said that he would have changed tack a long time ago if it had been left up to him and the only reasons he hadn't were that they had agreed to stick to the plan and that he had no new ideas. Steven's mother seemed almost resigned to the fact that Steven had some kind of intractable illness and said she felt unable to help him further. Again, the discussion centred on the importance of consistently implementing a shared approach over a reasonable period of time. An analogy was made with the use of antidepressant medication; when someone first starts taking the pills there is no immediate effect, it takes some weeks for the levels of the drug to build up sufficiently to be able to begin to lift the depression. This does not mean that in the early stages the pills are doing no good at all. Reluctantly, Steven's parents agreed to persist with what they were doing. They also agreed to make a point of finding some time for each other and to try to get out for at least one evening together. When they returned for the following session they reported that Steven was doing a bit better with his eating and they were very proud that they had helped him gain a little weight. They found it easier to continue as they were now at last seeing some small improvement.

While we are trying to help parents to work out together

how best to tackle the problem, the anorexic voice often interrupts with such statements as 'I won't eat, you can't make me'; 'You are just trying to make me fat'; 'Can't you see that I am too fat'; 'I hate you and I will never speak to you again'; 'If you make me eat all that I will run away and I'll kill myself.'

You will find that the more determined you become to overcome the illness, the more panic-stricken becomes the anorexia. The threats are often frightening but in our experience are hardly ever carried out. Sometimes the person with anorexia nervosa will not speak to her parents, as if to punish them. However, if you persevere with an approach that is consistent between you both and consistent over time, and you refuse to get caught up in arguing with the anorexic voice, you will notice gradual change and improvement.

Our work in the clinic, therefore, is to help you to find an approach with which you do feel comfortable and that you can apply consistently over time. We also help you to talk with your real child rather than the anorexic voice. As she re-emerges, you will be able to talk with her in detail about the worries that may have contributed to her illness. Some of the discussions we would have would be with just you as parents, some with you and your child, and some even with your other children as well. This is because the anorexia will inevitably be having an effect on every single member of the family and there may be aspects of family life that can sometimes keep the anorexia going. One very common misconception is that if we need to work with parents and families, that somehow means the family is to blame for the development of the disorder. We are very clear that this is not at all the case; rather, we work with the whole family because we know that anorexia nervosa is a very complicated, clever and deceptive disorder. It is too big a thing for your child to be able to tackle on her own and she will need the help and support of her parents and the rest of the family. It is very important at some stage to involve all members of the family, even younger brothers and sisters. They too can be affected by the anorexia, and they can play their own part in their sibling's recovery.

Shelley was twelve when she developed anorexia nervosa. She had a fourteen-year-old brother, Tony, and a four-year-old sister, Fay. Shelley's eating disorder was quite severe; she had lost a lot of weight and eventually required a hospital admission. Regular meetings were held with Shelley's parents alone, as well as with Shelley, her brother and her parents together. Tony did not always come because it was awkward for him to miss school, but when he did attend he contributed to the discussion and helped to bring some of the issues the family were struggling with out into the open. Shelley's little sister Fay did not come to the meetings; the family lived some distance away and she was looked after at home by her grandmother.

Some way into treatment, while Shelley was still in hospital, the therapist asked after Fay. Shelley's mother said that she was becoming quite concerned as they had been experiencing a number of problems with her. Her father added that it was all they needed, another daughter with problems. It became apparent that Fay was showing signs of regressed behaviour. She had been bedwetting, having tantrums and being generally difficult and stubborn, and had reverted to becoming extremely clingy and tearful when separated from her mother.

The therapist realized that she had omitted to involve Fay in the treatment process. On further questioning, and at a subsequent meeting when Fay did attend, it became clear that Fay was very worried and anxious about what was happening to her big sister. She had been told that Shelley was ill but she didn't seem to be behaving as if she was ill. Fay's understanding of being ill was that you wore your nightie and stayed in bed. Shelley seemed to be cross and sad when she saw her, and she did not understand why Shelley sometimes slept in her own bed and then kept disappearing. Fay's regressed behaviour was her way of expressing her worry and confusion.

Fay began to accompany her mother on some visits to see Shelley, and she came with her in the car when Shelley returned to the hospital after being at home for weekends. She knew where Shelley slept and drew her pictures to go on her wall. Shelley was very fond of her little sister and missed her very much. She was angry with her anorexia for getting in the way of their relationship and making her snappy and irritable with Fay. By including Fay in the work that Shelley was doing with the rest of her family's support, not only did

Fay's problems recede but Shelley seemed to find some new incentive and motivation to fight her eating disorder.

Parental counselling and family therapy form the mainstay of the treatment we offer, but there are other contributions. Many parents expect and want advice from a dietitian. This can often be helpful, providing that dietetic advice is offered within the context that it is only one component of management (see Chapters 4 and 5). Dietitians can advise what constitutes adequate intake or a balanced diet but many parents know this instinctively and may not need specialist dietetic advice. Sometimes it can be of great value to have a one-off appointment with a dietitian, because although many parents really do know what their children need they may have lost sight of this because of the long-standing nature of the eating problems. It can be helpful to be reminded and reassured. What is problematic is ensuring that your child eats what you provide.

What else might happen at a clinic? It is obviously helpful to know whether or not weight is being gained. The advantage of this being done in clinic is that the same accurate scales are used each time. Bathroom scales tend to be inaccurate and are much easier to manipulate in such a way that weight appears to have been gained when in fact it has not. You will already be aware that weighing is an emotionally fraught occasion. Many people with anorexia nervosa weigh themselves more than once a day, whereas others avoid weighing as much as possible. Yet others want to know their weight but do not want their parents to know, and some do not want to know their weight at all. It is very common indeed for weight to be manipulated to give an artificially high reading. The most popular technique to achieve this is 'water loading' (consuming large amounts of water shortly before weighing). This can be extremely dangerous. Alternative methods include concealing heavy objects in the underwear or leaning forward on the scales. People with anorexia nervosa invariably try these methods as a way of trying to convince whoever is responsible for them that they have gained weight.

Fortunately, knowing the weight at any one time is not

of any particular value, so if it has been artificially raised, this does not matter too much. It is only of value for weight to be considered in relation to previous recordings. The weight today does not mean anything very much but a weight chart that shows a gradual increase, or no change, or a fall off, over time, has obvious significance.

As you can see from Figure 3, a chart can show considerable fluctuations during a twelve-week period but very little change over time. Indeed, in this example there is overall only a 1 kg increase.

Figure 4 shows low water loading can make it look as though there has been an increase in weight. However, the apparent increase cannot be sustained and invariably the true weight shows through in time. In this case water loading was suspected and the child was reweighed after going to the toilet. There was a 1.5 kg difference.

More commonly, young people with anorexia nervosa show a fluctuating (or stepwise) increase in weight as they start recovering. This is demonstrated in Figure 5, in which there are five weeks when the weight has fallen from the previous week, and another five weeks when there has been no change from the previous week. Overall, however, the weight increases from 25 kg to 30.5 kg in twenty-four weeks.

Naturally, you and your child will want to know what weight target is being recommended. This is more difficult to

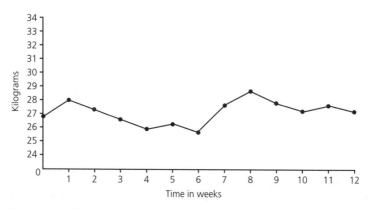

Figure 3 **No change in weight over time.**

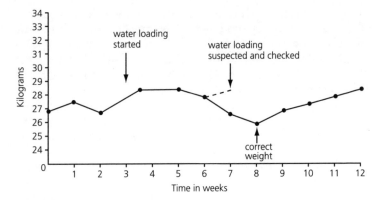

Figure 4 **Water loading.**

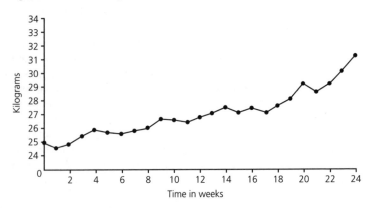

Figure 5 **Typical example of stepwise weight gain.**

ascertain than might be imagined. First, weight only has significance when considered in the context of height, age and gender. In general, the taller you are the more you will weigh, and until the age of about seventeen or eighteen weight increases with age. Generally, boys are likely to weigh more than girls. It is possible to determine a healthy weight within a certain range as determined by age, height and gender. The way this will usually be expressed is in terms of weight/height ratios or body mass index (BMI). If the person you are seeing uses these terms and you are not clear what they mean, do ask for them to be explained. Even if a healthy weight range is specified, we can't be certain that this range is right for any one individual or which point within the range represents the best weight for your child, because there is considerable variation between individuals. The majority of the population has a weight/height ratio of somewhere between 90 and 110 per cent and will be healthy within this range. However, we have seen children and teenagers who have been obviously unwell with a weight/height ratio of 112 per cent and have only recovered good health with a weight/height ratio of 120 per cent. Conversely, we have seen other children and teenagers who seem to have been perfectly healthy with a weight/height ratio as low as 80 per cent. In consequence, we can never be certain in advance as to what constitutes a healthy weight range for any one particular child.

Fortunately, there is a very reliable indicator of satisfactory weight in adolescent girls – pelvic ultrasound examinations (although regular menstruation is the best indicator!). It might seem strange that ultrasound can indicate that weight is satisfactory. However, there is a very good reason for this. The pelvic ultrasound shows clearly the shape, size and content of the ovaries and uterus. These can only be healthy when the weight is satisfactory. It is possible to determine from the shape, size and content of the ovaries and uterus whether they are indeed healthy and therefore whether the weight is OK. If they are immature for their age then the weight is too low; it is as simple as that. Once the ultrasound appearances are normal for age we know that a satisfactory weight has been achieved. Of course, it is still possible to estimate a healthy weight range and we will do so, but we emphasize that this is only an estimate.

There are two disadvantages to ultrasound. The first is that in pre-pubertal girls it cannot give as clear an indication of whether weight is satisfactory. This is because in this age group the ovaries and uterus haven't achieved full maturity – they are still developing. However, it can demonstrate that weight is too low by the presence of ovaries and uterus that are immature for age.

The second disadvantage is that there is a time lag of about two to three months from the point at which a healthy weight is achieved to the time when this is reflected on ultra-sound appearance. In practice, therefore, we estimate a healthy weight range and, two to three months after this has been achieved, we repeat the ultrasound to ensure pelvic organ maturity.

We may carry out other investigations, depending upon what has been done previously. If no detailed investigations have been conducted we will do these, and even if they have been done before we may repeat them in case there has been some physical deterioration. They also form a useful baseline upon which to evaluate progress during treatment.

Many children and teenagers with anorexia nervosa need some individual sessions where they can see someone on their own to help support them or explore underlying psychological issues. The nature of this one-to-one work may vary considerably from one clinic to another, and indeed from one therapist or clinician to another. The aim, however, is to assist in the process of returning your child to good health, by helping her manage the concerns she has around eating well enough to gain weight and getting to grips with the underlying problems. In almost all cases, people with anorexia nervosa have low self-esteem; they dislike them-selves and are ashamed of themselves. They consider that they are bad people and that eating is disgusting. When they look at themselves in the mirror they see a fat person whom they dislike intensely. Such distorted perceptions clearly need skilled help and indicate just how much more anorexia nervosa is than simply a wish to lose weight.

As described in earlier chapters, people with anorexia nervosa feel good about losing weight because of the sense of pride, achievement, control and well-being, as well as no longer feeling full or nauseated. A useful component of ther-apy is that focused on enhancing their motivation to recover (this is called motivational enhancement therapy, or MET). This approach is based on eliciting and acknowledging all the good things they feel about their anorexia; these feelings are not challenged and their value to the child is acknow-ledged. In the early stages of the illness children will only be able to acknowledge good things about being low weight, and won't accept that they are ill. With support and understanding they gradually become more able to accept that they are thin, but will not be willing to regain weight. Later they accept the need to regain weight, as they are more able to recognize the disadvantages as well as the advantages, but they are too frightened to try. Eventually, when they are able to perceive that the disadvantages outweigh the advantages, they start eating sufficiently to gain weight.

It is important to remember that, whatever form of individual therapy is offered, regular support for you as parents is essential. If resources are insufficient to provide both then we believe it is best to provide family counselling, thus ensuring that all get help.

In our clinics we also run support groups, both for the children and teenagers with anorexia nervosa, and for their parents. The parents in particular find these valuable in that they offer an opportunity for parents to meet with others in the same situation. They are able to exchange experiences, offer mutual support and provide ideas for tackling problems. The children's support groups are often centred on an activity such as art or drama. Children seem to prefer this way of communicating to straight talking and are often able to explore more difficult issues in this way.

Sometimes, the eating disorder is so severe that despite intensive treatment on an outpatient basis admission to hospital is required. This may be indicated by relentless weight loss, very poor circulation (with discoloured and cold feet and hands or sores that don't heal), very low blood pressure, irregular heart rhythm or abnormalities on blood tests. In addition, hospitalization may eventually be necessary if outpatient treatment hasn't worked after several months, even if the physical state is not dangerous. It is unwise to allow a child or teenager to stay at a low weight for too long because of the potential for long-term damage to the body.

If your child does need hospitalization this should ideally be in a unit that specializes in children or adolescents with eating disorders. Unfortunately, there are very few of these around and it is more likely that she would be admitted to a general paediatric ward or a general child or adolescent psychiatric unit. In the absence of a specialized unit, our preference would be for admission to a paediatric ward if there are physical complications, when the emphasis should be on reversing these and refeeding. If her physical state is reasonable and the admission is because of failed out-patient treatment then it would be better for the admission to be to a psychiatric unit geared to her age.

Skilled and experienced nurses are usually able to help people with anorexia nervosa to resume eating. It does take time, patience and understanding to help when there is so much dread attached. The principles are the same as those outlined in Chapters 4 and 5. It is probably easier in hospital because there are more adults around to share the burden, and often the other children can provide support and encouragement. In addition it is possible to provide more intensive treatment in hospital. For example, each young person would have allocated to them key nurses who between them would be available on a daily basis to provide intensive individual support. Group support and counselling are also available on a daily basis and the friendships made with the peer group are often a crucial part of the recovery process.

Occasionally, however, it is necessary to use artificial means to ensure adequate calorie intake. The most common of these is the use of nasogastric tube feeding. This is nothing like as unpleasant as some people believe. It involves gently passing a very narrow tube up the nose and down into the stomach. It is slightly uncomfortable when being passed but not painful and, once in place, there is no discomfort. High-calorie feeds are then passed down the tube. This procedure is in common use in hospitals for a wide range of different problems, of which anorexia nervosa is but one. Nearly all children and teenagers with anorexia nervosa give their consent to nasogastric tube feeding when this is deemed necessary, and the vast majority eventually express relief that this action was carried out.

Samantha, twelve, had been admitted to hospital after eighteen months of outpatient treatment had failed to help her eat adequately. Despite intensive and skilled nursing care she still refused to eat anything but minimal amounts. The ward staff discussed with

Samantha and her parents the options available. These included per-severing with the regular treatment programme, transferring her to another unit or nasogastric tube feeding. Samantha sullenly stated that she would not have a tube and would rather go elsewhere. Her parents opted for tube feeding on the grounds that she had been of very low weight for nearly two years and they were worried about the long-term damage. They doubted that another unit would have any more success without a tube.

Samantha was given the choice of who would pass the tube, where this would be done and who would be with her. The combin-ation of her having these choices, and all the adults responsible for her being in agreement about the most appropriate course of action, was sufficient for her to acquiesce. Samantha allowed the tube to be passed without fuss and made no attempt to remove it. She needed to be tube fed for several months before she was able to start eating normally.

Some years later, when she had made a good recovery, she wrote to us saying how glad she was that we had used tube feeding rather than prolong her struggle:

I couldn't bring myself to eat although I knew I needed to and that eventually I would die if I didn't. It was such a relief when the responsibility was taken away from me.

Some people mistakenly equate nasogastric tube feeding with forced feeding. This is quite simply a misconception. Forced feeding is not used except in the direst circumstances and only as an emergency and life-saving measure. Permis-sion to do this would always be sought not only from the parents but also be obtained in a court of law. Even then, every effort would be made to help the child or teenager to agree to the procedure. Between us we have been responsible for the care of several hundred young people with anorexia nervosa and only twice have we had to pass a tube without the child's agreement.

The question of the use of medication is often raised. We generally don't find medication particularly helpful in ano-rexia nervosa. Sometimes depression is prominent but this usually lifts with refeeding. If this does not happen then antidepressants may help. Tranquillizers and sedatives have very little part to play. Just occasionally a child may be so anxious and tormented by her dread of weight gain that a short course of tranquillizers may help. There have been some vociferous claims for the value of zinc and other natural substances but unfortunately there is absolutely no evidence that they are of any help. Indeed, the feeds that are given by tube are rich in zinc but they don't seem to speed up the recovery process. Some clinicians use calcium supplements to protect against osteoporosis, but we don't yet know how useful this is. Hormonal treatment such as oestrogens should be reserved for particularly intractable situations and it is best to avoid giving these to young people who are or should be still growing.

In summary, the treatment offered for anorexia nervosa needs to be comprehensive and intensive, with attention being paid to both physical and psychological treatments. The adults must take responsibility for ensuring adequate calorie intake whilst ensuring consistency between each other and over time. Every effort should be made to help the young person to build up her self-esteem, for poor self-esteem is what underlies anorexia nervosa.

Bulimia nervosa

The treatment of bulimia nervosa has both similarities to and differences from that of anorexia nervosa. The initial assessment and investigations are likely to be similar. Because vomiting is so common in bulimia nervosa it is important to check for changes in the blood chemistry, such as low levels of potassium. Therefore blood tests may well be carried out quite frequently. Also, ultrasound examination of the ovaries may be carried out because bulimia nervosa is often associated with the development of polycystic ovaries (see Chapter 3 and Glossary).

The mainstay of treatment is once more providing support and advice, both to parents and the young person, and will usually involve active attempts to structure eating patterns and reduce bingeing and purging episodes. You will need to know what you can do to help your child to resist the common and powerful urges to binge and purge. Whoever is seeing you in the clinic should be concentrating on this aspect of the problem. It is vital to avoid getting into any fights with your child, and hopefully the clinician will help you with this (see Chapters 4 and 5). Joining with your child in the fight against the eating disorder is absolutely essential; fighting her will only make the problem worse. As discussed in Chapters 4 and 5, you will need to help your child to find strategies to use when she feels compelled to binge or purge, and to help her identify the things that tend to lead to a binge.

Evelyn, fifteen, had been bingeing and purging for six months. Initially her parents had not realized, but her mother became suspicious of the amount of time Evelyn would spend in the bathroom after meals and then found a large number of crisp packets and chocolate wrappers in the dustbin. She asked Evelyn what was happening but Evelyn angrily denied anything and indicated that she wanted just to be left alone. Thereafter, whenever Evelyn went to the bathroom her mother would stand outside the bathroom door and listen. Evelyn became increasingly angry and secretive.

The strategy of spying and confronting certainly didn't work. The family counsellor who met Evelyn and her parents suggested that Evelyn should let her parents know what they could do that would help. At first Evelyn found it difficult to think of anything but, with encouragement, was able to say that she wanted them not to get angry but to be more understanding. Her father found this particularly hard, as he didn't understand. The counsellor reiterated that eating disorders are not logical and therefore are very hard to understand. He should not look for logic but should rather support Evelyn as best he could. Eventually they worked out some strategies for resisting the urge to binge. It transpired that Evelyn was most likely to binge when she was feeling low or bored. It was agreed that when this happened she would tell her mother, who would attempt to engage her in other activities such as listening to some music together or watching some TV. Evelyn's father, who was a keen jogger, offered to go running with her. Her mother was uncertain about this because she feared it would lead to compulsive exercising. Evelyn responded by criticizing her mother for being controlling and said she would like to do that. The counsellor advised that they try this combination for three weeks and then review it. There was indeed some improvement and it was decided to persevere. Gradually, over the months, the whole situation improved.

Parental or family counselling is likely to play an important part in the treatment offered but individual therapy has also been found to be very helpful in bulimia nervosa. The type of therapy most commonly used is known as cognitive behavioural therapy or CBT. This treatment is based on the assumption that the bingeing behaviour is associated with certain cognitions or thoughts. These thoughts are usually negative statements about the self, which are related to distress and low self-esteem. Put very simply, CBT attempts to monitor the behaviour and challenge the underlying thoughts and assumptions, with the aim of changing both. This can be harder than it may seem, as often the bingeing behaviour has become an entrenched or habitual response.

CBT for bulimia nervosa will usually involve meeting a therapist on a regular basis, once every week or two. The focus will be on identifying what is happening and when, what triggers the compulsions to binge and purge, and working out strategies for overcoming these. Attention is also paid to how the person with bulimia tends to think about and evaluate herself. Individuals are challenged in terms of their negative thoughts about themselves and are helped to re-evaluate themselves. In this way low self-esteem will usually be on the agenda and the therapist will be working with the individual to try to revise the thoughts and beliefs that sustain the negative self-image, and ultimately the bulimic behaviours. This, in combination with paying detailed attention to what is actually happening with the bingeing and purging behaviours, has proved a most effective way of working with people with bulimia nervosa, and is widely used.

Medication does have more of a part to play in bulimia nervosa than anorexia nervosa. There is increasing support for the use of fluoxetine (better known as Prozac) as a means of reducing the urge to binge. It appears to work by correcting an abnormality of neurotransmitters (chemical messengers) in the brain cells. Prozac has had both good and bad publicity and in reality is neither as awful nor as wonderful as various media reports have implied. When used in the right circumstances and correct dosage it can be helpful.

There are other drugs, similar to fluoxetine, which may be used instead.

Depression is not an uncommon accompaniment of bulimia nervosa and when this does occur the use of anti-depressants, usually one of the selective serotonin re-uptake inhibitors (SSRIs, which include fluoxetine and related compounds) might be considered.

Finally, a number of self-help manuals have recently been published (see Further Reading) and the person you are consulting may suggest that you try one of these. The manuals tend to be aimed more at adults attempting to manage their own eating disorder but they may also prove of help for younger people with bulimia nervosa.

Selective eating

As outlined in Chapters 4 and 5, there is usually no need for intensive or lengthy treatment of selective eating. The most important role for the clinician is to confirm the correct diagnosis and check that your child is healthy. This is done by taking full details about the problem, carrying out a careful physical examination, checking physical growth and development and possibly conducting some of the tests mentioned earlier in this chapter.

Most children do not want treatment for selective eating. As this type of eating behaviour is, in the majority of cases, relatively harmless and tends to resolve during the teenage years, there is often little point in trying to impose treatment. Coercion undoubtedly makes things worse and should be avoided. You should be wary of any clinician who does try to impose treatment for selective eating against your child's wishes if it has been established that she is not suffering ill effects in terms of her physical health. First, there is no need and, second, it may make things worse. The best time to offer treatment is when your child wants it and not before then. Many children, especially as they enter adolescence, become sufficiently embarrassed by the restrictions their eating habits impose to ask for help. This is a good time to respond.

However, even if your child is not suffering any ill effects physically, selective eating can sometimes lead to major disruptions to family and social life, resulting in social isolation and stresses and strains in family and other relationships. If your child has selective-eating problems, you will be the best judge of when the knock-on effects of your child's eating behaviour represent a real problem and when they do not. If you feel that they do then you should seek help, as well as trying to expand your child's repertoire as described in Chapters 4 and 5.

The most helpful approach offered by clinicians is a combination of individual work and parental counselling. The individual work will probably focus on helping your child to become more receptive to the idea of trying new foods. The therapist might discuss with him (most selective eaters are boys) which foods to try, in what amounts, when, where and with whom. Usually there will be only one new food tried at a time, in very small quantities, possibly starting with just a taste. The process is usually very slow and taken only at a pace the child can tolerate.

Individual therapy that focuses on the past or the 'subconscious' is of little value for this condition and should not be offered. It is not an effective use of time and resources in this context and its inevitable failure will be demoralizing for all concerned.

Parental counselling focuses on helping you support your child's efforts, allaying your anxieties and, as with all the eating disorders, adopting a consistent approach, both between yourselves and over time. You should be advised never to force your child, nor to punish if no progress is made, but the imaginative use of rewards and incentives can usually help to keep up the momentum.

Wayne, ten, had always been a picky eater. He had been difficult to wean and had preferred a very narrow range of foods from an early age. At first his parents considered this to be just a normal phase of food faddiness. However, it persisted into his school years and school lunches proved very difficult. This problem was overcome by his always taking peanut-butter sandwiches with him to school. The only other foods he ate were cornflakes, plain crisps and cheese slices; he would drink milk and water but nothing else.

Assessment confirmed the diagnosis of selective eating and that his physical health was perfectly satisfactory. He made it very clear that he didn't want to try new foods despite his parents' pleas. When techniques for tackling the problem were discussed he became very distressed. It was quite evident that he wasn't ready to accept any help and that such efforts were likely to meet with resistance at best, and possibly deterioration. His parents found it hard to accept our advice but felt they had little choice. They had previously noticed that when they tried to introduce new foods Wayne became distressed for several days on end, and was as adamant as ever that he would not eat anything new or different.

Two years later they returned because Wayne had asked for help. His friends were teasing him and he had been unable to go on a school skiing trip to France because his favoured foods would not have been available. Reassessment showed that he had continued to grow at the normal rate for his age and that his physical health was excellent. Wayne somewhat sheepishly said that he wanted to try to eat some other foods ' 'Cos I'm fed up with being different from other kids'.

Arrangements were made for Wayne to see a therapist, who was able to help him draw up a timetable for trying out certain new foods. They also discussed the quantities, who he would prefer to prepare and serve them and who would be with him when he tried them. He decided to start with jam sandwiches and if that worked he would then try chocolate spread. Wayne also offered to try a new drink and opted for apple juice, which he had drunk a few times in the past, but never consistently. He decided that he would ask his mother to be with him for the jam sandwiches and his father for the chocolate spread. He didn't want his brother or sister around during these attempts. His parents were disappointed that his choices were so limited but the parent counsellor reminded them that he had to be supported at his own pace.

Wayne managed gradually to increase his range of foods and drinks and, as time went by, the pace increased. Within six months of treatment starting he was able to stay overnight with friends and had been on a weekend school trip to London.

Restrictive eating

Restrictive eating can be very difficult to treat and, like selective eating, is best left alone unless physical well-being is at risk. The doctor will arrange for a full assessment and investigations. Usually the child is physically well, in which case no treatment would be offered.

If, however, physical health is compromised, as shown by physical examination or investigations, then treatment is indicated. We find that the easiest way of making progress is to bring such children into hospital. Sometimes just a change of environment is sufficient to allow for a better dietary intake. This may or may not persist after discharge from hospital. If it does, well and good; if not, then it may be necessary to explore in more depth what may be contributing towards the child's continuing inadequate food intake or delay in growth. A small number of children are for one reason or another not able to thrive in their home environment. This can be for many different reasons, sometimes related to the home situation but sometimes related to the situation or events outside the home. If a child is unable to thrive at home this is a matter of some concern, and careful consideration will need to be given to ensure that the necessary steps are taken to ensure the child's well-being.

If there is no improvement in hospital and physical health is in jeopardy then a number of options may be considered. If your child is very short he may be treated with a short course of growth-hormone injections. These will stimulate both appetite and growth. Alternatively, but only if the child is fourteen or older, consideration may be given to the artificial induction of puberty by a course of hormones. These also are likely to stimulate the appetite and growth as well as bringing on puberty. Such decisions are complex and should only be made after considerable explanation and discussion with you and your child.

Angus, ten, had always been short and thin, with a very poor appetite. He was growing and putting on weight at an even rate, but was about four years delayed in his development (Figures 6 and 7).

Neither exploration of his past nor physical examination nor investigation revealed any obvious reason for his very poor appetite

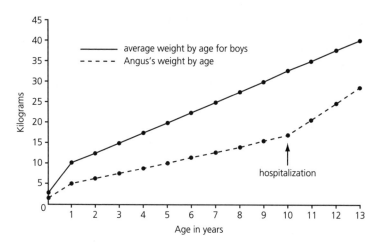

Figure 6 Angus's weight chart.

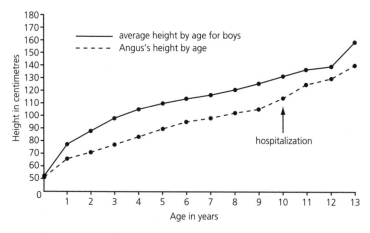

Figure 7 Angus's height chart.

and growth. He had received some psychotherapy when he was much younger.

Parental support and counselling on an outpatient basis had no positive effect and eventually Angus was admitted to an eating-disorders unit. Initially there was no change in his eating pattern but, after a few weeks during which he had become very friendly with a boy of his age, he expressed an interest in trying to eat more. This seemed to coincide with the friend being prepared for leaving hospital. Angus gradually increased his intake of food, but only by about 25 per cent. However, he did start to put on weight and it was decided to discharge him gradually. He started by spending weekends at home and then increasingly longer periods, including some visits to school. Eventually he was discharged, after which he continued to eat slightly more than prior to his hospitalization. His growth pattern improved, although remaining slow. He eventually entered puberty at the age of sixteen and his final height (aged eighteen) was 159 cm (5 foot 3 inches) and he remained thin. He decided to become a jockey so that he could take advantage of his small stature.

No cause was found for Angus's poor appetite and delayed growth. It is likely that he ate slightly better in hospital because of peer-group encouragement and intensive nursing attention, and fortunately he was able to retain this pattern after discharge. Had he not, then hormonal treatment would have been considered.

Food phobia

This can also be a difficult condition to treat and tends to cause much anxiety. As with all the other eating problems the basic principles of treatment are the same. The doctor will often first get full details of the problem, conduct a careful physical examination and carry out some investigations. Because children with food phobia have anxieties about and problems with swallowing, the tests may include investigation of the swallowing mechanisms. Usually, however, no abnormalities are found. Sometimes 'reflux' is diagnosed. This is a not uncommon condition in which the muscle between the oesophagus (gullet) and the stomach is weak and allows stomach contents to return into the oesophagus. Sometimes this leads to vomiting. Your child may associate eating with the unpleasant consequence of vomiting and thus avoid eating or at least express fear or discomfort. More commonly in food phobia there has been a previously traumatic event, which has led to fears of swallowing, and there are no physical abnormalities (see Chapters 3, 4 and 5).

The decision on treatments will be based on a number of

factors. Are there any physical abnormalities? Is growth delayed? What fears does your child have about eating?

Any physical abnormalities will require specific treatment. For example, reflux is treated by specific medications that help speed up stomach emptying and protect the lining of the oesophagus from erosion by stomach acid. Problems with the swallowing mechanism are often treated by a speech therapist. Parents are often surprised by this but many speech therapists have a special expertise in this area.

The concerns about taste and texture and fears of vomiting, choking or suffocating are best treated by a cognitive therapist. The therapist will start with teaching your child some relaxation techniques. It is vital to allay the associated anxiety as it is impossible to be both anxious and relaxed at he same time. Thus the relaxation plays an essential part in the treatment. The actual techniques used will depend upon your child's age and this will also help determine whether or not you are present.

Peter was twelve and had recently started at secondary school. He developed a food phobia following an incident at school. A boy two years older had started choking and been unable to breathe at the lunch table. This boy had a serious nut allergy and had inadvertently eaten something that contained ground peanuts. The boy had been rushed to hospital and had nearly died. The whole situation was extremely alarming to Peter, who had been present in the dining hall and had witnessed the older boy's immediate allergic reaction; he had already been finding it quite stressful settling in at school and he developed a fear that he had allergies that he might not yet know about.

Peter's anxiety levels were very high at mealtimes, especially at school or when he ate away from home. He was frightened and sometimes tearful, and found it hard to swallow. He felt sick and as if he had a hard knot in his stomach. This took away his appetite, so that he ate very little. The therapist worked with Peter on relaxation skills. The way Peter found worked best was to use the 'old green armchair method'.

The therapist first talked with Peter about his likes and dislikes, about his interests and hobbies, and about the sorts of things that made him feel good and the sorts of things that made him feel anxious (besides eating). She identified that he loved cycling, was a great fan of the Asterix books and liked watching television. She asked Peter to make himself comfortable in his chair and to close his eyes. First, they just concentrated on feeling comfortable, and slowing breathing down a bit. Then the therapist asked Peter to imagine he was going through a door, which led to a flight of stairs going down to a basement. The basement was warm, with soft lights, and in it was a television and a big comfortable old green armchair. She invited Peter to switch the television on and start to watch his favourite programme. All the time the therapist was reminding Peter how comfortable and relaxed he felt. After the programme a bicycle appeared on the screen, which, as it was a magic television in a magic room, Peter was invited to get on. The therapist asked him to imagine climbing out of the chair on to the bicycle on the screen. The bicycle took him on a ride (which involved the things Peter had said he most liked about riding his bike) to Asterix's village, and more particularly to the druid Getafix's house. Getafix gave Peter a small amount of one of his magic potions to drink. Peter was asked to imagine the potion slipping easily down his throat. It was a magic potion that would protect him and keep him safe if he should eat anything that he might be allergic to. After drinking the potion, the bicycle took him back, and he was asked to climb back out of the television. He was then asked to climb slowly back up the stairs from the basement and open his eyes again when he felt ready. The therapist then discussed with Peter how he felt, and asked him to try taking himself on the same journey before mealtimes. They had a conversation with Peter's mother to let her know that Peter had some 'homework' and that he would need a quiet space for a few minutes before mealtimes.

The following session Peter came back. He had been trying the green armchair method with some success. He was eager to tell the therapist how he had changed the story a bit. He found that he could do it quite quickly and that it was helping him feel much less anxious and tense at mealtimes.

Once relaxation is achieved, similar methods are used to those applied for selective eating (see above). Occasionally, medication to aid relaxation may be indicated. One particular medication, alprazolam (Xanax), has been found to be particularly helpful.

Food avoidance emotional disorder

The assessment and treatment of this condition has much in common with anorexia nervosa. The physical complications may sometimes be just as severe. The general principles of management should be applied regardless. Perhaps the main difference in treatment from anorexia nervosa is that medication is more likely to be used. If depression is prominent then antidepressants are useful. Those most likely to be used include fluoxetine, fluvoxamine, sertraline, amitryptyline and imipramine. When obsessive-compulsive symptoms are prominent the most useful medications include clomipramine and fluoxetine. Severe anxiety, if unrelieved by relaxation techniques (see Peter, above), may need medication. Amitriptyline is often useful in such cases, and occasionally diazepam may be needed.

Parents are often concerned about the use of medication, believing it may lead to addiction or have harmful side effects. The reality is that only diazepam of all the medications mentioned can lead to dependency. This only occurs when it is used for long periods of time in moderate to large doses. When prescribed for children and teenagers with anxiety related to eating disorders, it would normally only be used in small doses for very short periods of time. The risk of addiction in such cases is minuscule.

Side effects of the other medications are common but generally minor. Any medication can cause some drowsiness, stomach upsets and skin rashes. Some can cause constipation, dry mouth or blurred vision. All these side effects tend to be short-lived, usually disappearing after a week or two. They can often be avoided by starting with very low doses and slowly building up the dose. This has the advantage of reducing the likelihood of side effects but the disadvantage of taking longer to have a beneficial effect. In making decisions about the use of such medication, the benefits and risks have to be balanced. In general, when medication is indicated in early-onset eating disorders the benefits considerably outweigh the risks. It is important to emphasize that medication is not used unless there are strong indications for so doing, such as in food avoidance emotional disorder or to treat the severe and persisting depression associated with anorexia nervosa.

Compulsive overeating

This is another condition that is very hard to treat. As stated in the previous chapter, the principles of treatment have much in common with bulimia nervosa. The main difference between the two conditions is that compulsive overeaters do not have a major preoccupation with their weight and shape, and therefore do not try to control their weight by purging.

Investigations hardly ever reveal any physical cause for the overeating. In other words, the excess eating is not due to 'faulty glands'. There are only a couple of conditions in which there is a definite physical cause. These are relatively easily recognized by the fact that such children tend to be very delayed in their learning and usually also very short.

Treatment should not focus too heavily on dietary restriction. This rarely seems to work and instead gives the child a sense of failure. Nor are there any medications that have any value in such situations. It is far more useful to consider the techniques associated with the management of bulimia nervosa, most particularly focusing on issues of self-esteem. Motivational enhancement therapy, as described earlier in the treatment of anorexia nervosa may also be useful in increasing the motivation to manage weight.

Melissa, fifteen, had always had a ravenous appetite. At first her parents were able to control her weight by restricting her intake but as she got older she started to raid the food cupboard and fridge. Later she started stealing money to buy sweets, chocolates and cakes. As she became considerably overweight, so she became more isolated at school. She dealt with her distress by comfort eating.

When referred to a specialist Melissa was 70 per cent over-weight. Previous attempts to get her to diet had all failed and there seemed no point in setting up another failure. Instead, she was offered some individual therapy, which focused on her low self-esteem and inability to make and sustain friendships. As Melissa gained confidence in her therapist she became able to express her sadness and despair. The therapist supported her through this very painful 'self-exposure' over a period of three to four months. Gradually they started exploring what went wrong for Melissa when she tried to make friends and devising techniques that she could try. They would evaluate these in the next meeting. After about six months Melissa told her therapist with joy that she had been invited to stay over at a friend's house. This was the first such invitation. No effort had been made to help her directly with weight loss, but she did manage to lose several kilograms during the year after therapy started. She was still overweight but no longer 'stood out'.

The key to the relative success of Melissa's treatment was working not on dietary restriction but on self-esteem and problem solving.

Clearly there are similarities and differences in the treatments of the different early-onset eating disorders. The general principles outlined in previous chapters hold true throughout, but there are some treatments that are specific to one disorder and not indicated in others. For this reason it is important to ensure the correct diagnosis. Not all clinicians are going to be familiar with the range of eating disorders in this age group, let alone their treatments. It is best, therefore, to seek the help of a specialist. If you are in doubt as to whether your child's problem has been correctly diagnosed or treated, you should not hesitate to say so. Good clinicians will always be open to such questions and challenges and will be prepared to discuss openly with you all aspects of your child's problems and their management. If they are not, then you may wish to seek a further opinion and you can always show them this book to explain your own reasoning.

7

What about the future?

Any parent of a child with an eating disorder is bound to have concerns about the future and what it holds for their child. In this chapter we describe what can happen and summarize current knowledge on which factors influence outcome. As there are differences between each of the eating disorders, we will discuss each in turn. However, it is important to be aware of the fact that recovery is likely to be gradual rather than sudden. Indeed, it can be a painfully slow process with many setbacks on the way. The associated frustrations can in themselves create problems and to avoid these you are likely to need the patience of a saint. However, if you apply the various principles outlined in earlier chapters your child will have a better chance of ultimately making a good recovery.

Anorexia nervosa

Of all the eating disorders, anorexia nervosa is one of the hardest to overcome and probably has the least satisfactory long-term outlook. However, it is by no means all bad news; indeed, the long-term outlook is good providing certain things happen (these are described later). Generally, about two-thirds of all children and adolescents with anorexia nervosa will eventually make a good and sustained recovery. This means that not only do they maintain a healthy weight but that they also experience regular periods, achieve satisfactory physical health, lose their preoccupation with weight and shape, gain self-esteem, and lead normal lives.

Of the remaining third, the majority makes a partial recovery. This usually involves them having persisting concerns with weight and shape, with subsequent avoidance of a satisfactory diet and maintenance of a somewhat low weight, with irregular or absent periods. However, in many other ways they lead a relatively normal existence, with satisfactory social lives, employment and even long-term relationships.

A small minority of young people with anorexia nervosa, perhaps around 5 per cent, remains very unwell for several years. This usually involves their maintaining a very low weight with all the unhealthy physical consequences. They have persisting and severe preoccupations around weight and shape, and continuing low self-esteem. They may well require one or more hospital admissions. A few develop bulimia nervosa and others may develop other psychiatric disorders such as depression or anxiety.

Finally, a small number of young people will die. Deaths are very rare in children and adolescents with anorexia nervosa, but they can occur. The cause of death is usually either related to the consequences of starvation or persistent vomiting; alternatively, it can be the result of suicide. In the fourteen or so years we have been working with children with eating disorders, only one child has died out of the many hundreds we have seen. A child's death is a tragic event, and one death is one too many. It is important to remember that anorexia nervosa can be fatal, and that it is a serious condition whose progress must be checked. Although it is distressing to think that your child could ultimately die from her eating disorder, this *is* the reality of anorexia nervosa and you might use this knowledge to strengthen your resolve to fight it.

It is important to emphasize that the recovery process is almost invariably slow and gradual. Very few people with anorexia nervosa suddenly lose all their concerns and start eating normally. We expect little change during the first month of outpatient treatment, and even in hospital improvement can be painfully slow. Usually, during the second month of treatment we note an improvement in dietary intake and a gradual weight gain. We have used the term 'improvement in dietary intake' deliberately because this is different from resuming normal eating patterns and behaviour. Indeed, these often do not occur for several weeks or even months. This does *not* matter so long as your child is eating sufficiently to gain weight. The main concern in the early stages of treatment should be sufficient intake each day. It really does not matter how, when or where this is done. Most people with anorexia nervosa retain an irregular eating pattern for some time after they have started taking adequate amounts over each 24-hour period.

Natasha, fifteen, had started eating again after her family had consulted a clinician. However, she insisted on eating alone in her room and having meals at times of her choosing rather than at regular mealtimes. After a few days, her father insisted she should eat with the family and she immediately stopped eating completely. At a further consultation with the clinician it was agreed that she should be supported in finding her own way and pace, and only if she didn't gain weight should this policy be changed. Fortunately she did gain weight and after about six weeks she asked her mother to join her during meals, and later her sister. It was several months before she could manage eating in her father's presence but he was able to accept the advice despite his own reservations about it. Natasha made a good recovery over the next year.

So long as you help your child to eat adequately over each 24-hour period then any irregular pattern does not matter. Indeed, if you do try to impose a particular pattern then your child is quite likely to slip back to an inadequate total intake, as shown in Natasha's case. It is far better to tolerate whatever pattern she adopts as long as the intake is adequate. Nor does it matter at this stage what sort of food she eats, so long as it is adequate to ensure sufficient weight gain.

Following a couple of sessions of family therapy, Serena, sixteen, said that she would start eating again but only eggs, cheese, fruit, and salad. She also had milk drinks. Over a period of three months on this diet she gained 4 kg. Gradually thereafter she introduced new foods to her diet and eventually made a complete recovery.

Clearly we need to consider what determines whether or

not a young person with anorexia nervosa makes a good and sustained recovery. In our experience there are a number of vital factors:

- As parents you work well together as a team. You take a consistent approach to the management of your child's eating disorder, both between each other and over time. This involves both of you agreeing on how to tackle the problem, working out exactly what you are going to do and then supporting each other, as well as your child, for as long as it takes. Changing approaches too soon, or one parent taking a different approach from the other, is *very* likely to lead to deterioration rather than improvement.
- You can see that your child is distressed and not herself and you do not get into a habit of blaming her for her behaviour. You are able to accept that your child does not actively and willingly choose to be like this, but rather that she is a victim of the anorexia nervosa.
- You can tolerate stage two (see Chapters 4 and 5) and help your child to express painful and negative feelings without recrimination.

Parents have an understandable concern about the potential for long-term physical damage from anorexia nervosa. This can certainly occur in particular circumstances. Generally, however, there is little likelihood of permanent damage, providing recovery starts within a year of the onset of the illness. The main risk factors for physical damage include:

- low weight that persists for more than a year
- recurrent vomiting
- laxative misuse.

The problems that can occur in the early stages of the illness have been described in Chapter 3. Most of these reverse with weight gain. However, persisting low weight can cause irreversible damage in some circumstances. If the weight loss has persisted through the critical time for growth (i.e. eleven to fourteen for girls and thirteen to sixteen for boys), there may be a failure to catch up with linear growth; in other words, your child may never achieve her projected full-adult height. Similarly, if weight loss persists through the critical time for depositing minerals in the bones (i.e. fourteen to sixteen), the reduction in the thickness of the bones may not be reversible, leading to what is commonly known as brittle bones. When this occurs in a mild form it is called osteopenia, and in the more severe form, osteoporosis. This potentially severe complication emphasizes the importance of early recognition and treatment of anorexia nervosa.

Another complication of persistent low weight is regression of the ovaries and uterus to an immature stage of development. Generally these do return to normal, but if weight loss persists for many years it is possible that this may prove irreversible. It is not yet clear what length of time is critical.

Recurrent self-induced vomiting can lead to a number of long-term complications. The most problematic of these is the fact that the vomiting can take on a life of its own and occurs uninvited. This can be very difficult to treat. Persistent vomiting can also lead to bleeding and ulceration in the oesophagus, as well as contributing to the development of cysts in the ovaries. Sometimes these can become infected, bleed or rupture.

Laxative abuse can cause the lower bowel to lose its tone, with consequent long-lasting constipation. This is generally reversible, but requires skilled treatment. Longstanding laxative abuse can also lead to blood loss, severe pain and a lifetime of gastrointestinal complaints.

Fortunately, many of these long-term complications can be treated successfully but it is obviously best to ensure early treatment of the anorexia nervosa so that they do not occur at all.

Finally, it is important to know that about one in three young people with anorexia nervosa do suffer at least one relapse of their eating disorder. This usually occurs within the first year of apparent recovery, but may occur at any time during the following five years, and sometimes after an even longer period free of anorexia. It is not yet clear why some but not others relapse. In general, we believe those who do relapse are those in whom the criteria mentioned above for making a full and sustained recovery were not fulfilled.

Many of those whom we know to have relapsed are also those who have failed to complete stage two (see p. 82).

Gina, twelve, seemed to be making a reasonable recovery from anorexia nervosa. As she developed a more assertive and adolescent mode of relating to her parents, they in turn became less tolerant of her eating disorder and told her off for being rude and defiant. After one particularly difficult episode in which she shouted obscenities at her parents, she was not allowed to see or phone her friends for a week. This did not initially appear to inhibit her recovery and her parents were pleased to note that she seemed to return to her previously pleasant and perfectionist personality. The family therapist expressed concern that her parents had inhibited her from going through stage two, but they were only too pleased 'to have our old Gina back'. Eight months later Gina relapsed and seemed to go back to square one. It was some time before her parents could accept that they had to allow her to go completely through stage two.

Finally, some young people are, for one reason or another, unable to begin to verbalize their distress. Such children may, as it were, go through the motions of recovering but will not have addressed many of the important issues that contributed to the development and maintenance of their eating disorder. Their vulnerability to relapse will be high in the face of continuing or new stressful factors in their environment.

In summary, recovery from anorexia nervosa can be complete and sustained, and is in the majority of cases. It does seem possible to improve the likelihood of this happening by trying to fulfil the conditions we have outlined.

Bulimia nervosa

Research indicates that the outlook for sufferers of bulimia nervosa seems to be quite good when they are treated by specialists. With specifically designed treatments such as cognitive behavioural therapy, there is a significant reduction in bingeing and purging in as many as 85 per cent of adult patients. The use of medication to supplement this treatment may enhance the results. We do not have equivalent information for younger patients. However, it is likely that results should be similar, provided that parents are involved in the treatment process.

Our clinical experience indicates that the same principles apply as for anorexia nervosa. In other words, you need to acknowledge that your child's eating disorder is a reflection of some degree of distress and does not represent deliberately difficult behaviour. You will need to work out together how best to handle the problems and form a team with your child in a battle against the bulimia nervosa. Your child may initially be very embarrassed and ashamed, and may find it difficult to be open with you about what she is doing. You will need to tolerate her emerging autonomy and rebellion as she learns to express her emotions and deal with difficult feelings in ways other than by bingeing and vomiting or abusing laxatives.

Remember that recovery will be gradual and that there will be ups and downs and persisting symptoms for some time to come. Relapse may well occur, and if so you should handle this in the same way as the original episode.

Long-term complications are mostly those associated with repeated vomiting and laxative abuse, as described in the section on anorexia nervosa earlier in this chapter.

Selective eating

Fortunately the outlook for selective eaters is really very good. Almost all such young people seem to grow out of the problem during their teenage years, if not earlier. A very small minority, probably fewer than 1 per cent, continue to be selective eaters into adult life. Interestingly, this does not seem to be too much of a problem to them, perhaps because adults generally have a wider range of strategies than do children for dealing with difficulties. We are not aware of any such children who have suffered any long-term consequences, whether or not they have grown out of it. However, we do see children who are finding it harder to overcome the problem than is necessary because their parents have adopted a coercive approach. This not only does not help but can actually make the situation worse. Generally, however, selective eaters do very well.

Restrictive eating

These children tend to remain poor eaters throughout child-hood but have improved appetites as they mature. Usually by adult life they are eating fairly satisfactorily. Commonly we discover that such children have at least one parent who was similar as a child. This suggests an inherited component. Restrictive eaters do tend to turn out to be thin adults, but not unhealthy.

Jack had caused his parents considerable anxiety throughout his pre-school years because he ate so poorly. The doctors who saw him could find nothing wrong and tried to reassure his parents, who however remained anxious. At school entry aged five, physical exam-ination showed that although Jack was below weight for his age he was growing normally. This pattern continued throughout his child-hood and adolescence, and at the age of eighteen he was 175 cm (5 foot 10 inches) but only weighed 64 kg (10 stone). His general health was fine.

The long-term complications of being of low weight as a consequence of eating less than most throughout childhood do not seem to be as severe as those of anorexia nervosa. The reason for this may be in part due to the fact that such people have naturally small appetites, and also that their weight does not drop as it does in anorexia nervosa. In other words, some children are naturally reasonably healthy despite a small dietary intake. Again, it is likely that this is genetic-ally determined. As most such children are boys we do not have any information on long-term effects on the ovaries and uterus. The most likely long-term problem is persisting distress around eating, as a result of coercion to eat.

Food phobia

As mentioned earlier, this is a difficult condition to over-come. Because it is relatively uncommon we do not have sufficient information on long-term outcome or effects. However, it is very rare in adults so it is likely that most children do indeed grow out of it. Any complications are likely to be similar to those that are a consequence of inadequate dietary intake, as in anorexia nervosa. As with the other eating disorders, persisting psychological problems can occur as a result of coercive approaches to eating. Food-phobic children are particularly susceptible to the adverse consequences of coercion.

Abe, eight, had vomited a few times as a result of a stomach infection. He became very anxious about eating solid foods and insisted on eating only soft foods and liquids. His father became very frustrated and forced him to eat some meat. Abe vomited immediately and for two days was unable to eat anything.

Food avoidance emotional disorder

At present, we do not know much about the outcome of this condition. However, the course of the disorder is likely to be similar to others in that recovery will be gradual with setbacks from time to time. Our experience is that if the general guidelines offered in this book are applied and the underlying troubles addressed, such children tend to make a good recovery.

Any complications are likely to be those associated with persisting low weight (see the section on Anorexia nervosa, p. 135), undue coercion or unresolved underlying emotional problems.

Compulsive overeating

This is probably the hardest of the eating disorders to overcome, yet no one understands why. Often these children genuinely seem to have very large appetites, which, combined with a slow metabolism, makes it easy to gain weight. This is all made more difficult by the fact that such children often resort to comfort eating whenever upset or bored. Sadly, no really effective treatments have been found as yet for these children and generally their problems persist into adult life.

Being mildly to moderately overweight is unlikely to cause serious long-term harm. However, being severely overweight can cause major physical problems and you will need to ensure that there is careful monitoring by a doctor.

Freddy was ten when his father died unexpectedly. Previously he had been a somewhat overweight boy with a large appetite, who was otherwise healthy. In the few months after his father's death he started eating vast quantities of junk food, including sweets and chocolates. Freddy was soon so overweight that he became breathless when walking around and required hospital admission to ensure weight loss. Within three weeks he had lost 6 kg and was breathing normally again. He was seen by a psychologist who helped him to talk in depth about his sadness and guilt in relation to his father's death. One year later he was back to his original weight, and although eating heartily and still overweight he was much happier.

Most overweight people live perfectly happy, contented and useful lives. Provided they have not been made to feel bad about themselves, there is no reason why they should not cope perfectly satisfactorily.

Conclusions

The outlook for most sufferers of eating disorders is quite good, although much better for some than others. A good outcome is more likely if the right treatment is initiated early and if parents adopt a consistent and cooperative approach, avoiding blame and recriminations and accepting that the child has not chosen to have an eating disorder and is not just behaving in a wilful and difficult manner.

8

Case vignettes

Linda: Anorexia nervosa

Linda was the elder of two girls; her sister Sian was two and a half years younger. Her parents were in their early thirties when they started their family and both had successful careers, her mother as a feature writer for a national newspaper and her father a middle-grade civil servant. The family lived in the suburb of a large city and was reasonably prosperous. Her mother's parents lived relatively near; her father's parents lived about 100 miles away.

Linda had always been an apparently happy, popular and talented child. She had attended nursery school and later her local primary school with enthusiasm. Her teachers frequently commented on her energy and love of life. Linda always had many friends and led a very active social life. She loved animals and had two cats and a dog. She was enthusiastic about dancing and attended ballet classes on Saturdays.

At the age of eleven Linda took entrance exams and attended interviews for a number of schools with good reputations. She was offered places at each. Her parents chose the school with the best academic reputation and Linda seemed to settle happily there. Her school reports for the first two years were excellent and her year head predicted a very successful future. She decided to learn the clarinet and was an enthusiastic member of the under-thirteen's netball team.

Linda's health had always been good, apart from the usual childhood illnesses, and she was taller than average. Her first period occurred shortly before her thirteenth birthday. A year later the family were planning a summer holiday in France and Linda suggested that she, Sian and their mother should go shopping for suitable clothes.

Linda could not find anything she particularly liked and returned home somewhat despondent. The next day her mood seemed back to normal and the episode was forgotten. Two weeks later, three weeks before the holiday, Linda told her mother that she didn't have any summer clothes that fitted and that she didn't want to go on holiday. Her mother showed her several garments that she believed to fit and Linda seemed to accept this. The holiday proved rather less successful than had been expected. Linda did play tennis with her family most days but was otherwise somewhat withdrawn and at times quite morose, completely out of character for her. She refused to go swimming and often stayed indoors reading a book. Linda's parents attributed her change of behaviour to missing her friends and just normal teenage moodiness.

On her return home and to school, Linda seemed to revert to normal for a while. During the autumn months she discussed becoming a vegetarian and at Christmas refused to eat turkey. Thereafter she avoided all meat. The winter was particularly cold and Linda seemed to enjoy wearing thick woollen sweaters, which she refused to discard when the warmer spring weather arrived. Her mother thought she was eating rather less than usual but Linda adamantly denied this.

One evening Linda accused her father of preferring Sian to her – this was shortly after Sian had also gained entrance to Linda's school – and ran to her room in tears. Her mother went to Linda's room to comfort her and walked in just as Linda was undressing to go to bed. She was shocked to see just how thin Linda had become. She confronted Linda about this and asked her if she was anorexic. Linda yelled at her mother to mind her own business, burst into tears and hid beneath the bedclothes.

A few days later the family doctor saw Linda and said it was just a phase and suggested they see a dietitian. Although neither of Linda's parents was convinced, they agreed to do so. The dietitian gave Linda a talk about healthy eating and provided Linda's mother with a diet sheet. This made little difference and Linda's parents became increasingly concerned at Linda's low mood and poor eating. She was still doing well at school, getting good reports and grades, and working hard in the evenings on her homework. She also continued to go to ballet classes and play the clarinet.

One morning Linda's father woke up particularly early, went to the bathroom and was puzzled to see Linda's light on. He went into her room and discovered her doing homework. She was furious with him for barging in and refused to answer his questions. Linda's parents were now very concerned about her and returned to the family doctor. Again he said it was all just a phase and not atypical of adolescence. They said they wanted her to have a full check-up and asked for a referral to an eating-disorder specialist or a paediatrician. The family doctor said it was unlikely that Linda had anorexia but agreed to refer Linda to the local paediatrician.

Some weeks later, the paediatrician assessed Linda and confirmed that her weight was very low and that she had poor circulation to her hands and feet. Linda acknowledged that she had been feeling cold and dizzy, and that her periods had stopped some months previously. The paediatrician recommended that Linda should be admitted to hospital to help her gain weight. Linda pleaded with her parents that she should stay at home and promised to eat better. They all agreed to give it a two-week trial.

Initially Linda did appear to eat more, although she remained miserable and angry. After about eight days her parents noticed that she was spending a lot of time in the bathroom. They asked her about this and she denied it. Her mother thought she could smell vomit in the washbasin but Linda angrily denied that it was anything to do with her. Two days later a bag of discarded food was found under her bed.

On returning to see the paediatrician Linda's parents had determined that they wanted her admitted to hospital. The paediatrician agreed and Linda spent the next week in hospital, where she was seen by a child psychiatrist, who recommended some family therapy. The parents were a little surprised by this suggestion, as they hadn't thought that there were any problems in the family apart from Linda's eating disorder. The child psychiatrist explained that the purpose of the therapy would be to help the family find ways of fighting the illness.

Linda ate better in hospital, despite insisting that she was already overweight and didn't need to gain any more. She was discharged home after ten days; family therapy was due to start the next week. Over the weekend her parents had to work very hard to help Linda eat even small amounts. They disagreed with each other about how best to help her, with Linda's father wanting to be more coercive than her mother. There were many rows and Sian became increasingly upset, saying that she wanted to go and live with her granny. Linda's father insisted that her mother should accompany Linda to the bath-room, while Linda refused to have anyone in there. The weekend was a disaster and it was no surprise that when they met with the family therapist the next week Linda had lost more weight.

The family therapist spent most of the meeting discussing with Linda's parents how they were handling the problems. They acknow-ledged that they had different approaches and that they were often in disagreement. When the therapist tried to help them reach agree-ment, Linda commonly interrupted. The therapist didn't tell them what they should do, despite their repeated requests to her to do so. She simply focused on getting them to work out strategies for help-ing Linda with which they both felt comfortable. They kept trying to get the therapist to help them work out what had gone wrong for Linda, but she simply repeated that that was something they could do later, but at this stage the main concern was helping Linda to eat enough to survive.

The next few weeks were very difficult for everyone. Linda accused her parents of hating her 'You just want me to be a fat pig; if you really cared you wouldn't force food down me.' They in turn insisted that they loved her and weren't going to let her starve herself to death. They had by this time reached an agreement that they would take it in turns to sit with her at mealtimes, that they would encourage and support her in eating, but not force her to eat. How-ever, they made it clear that they would not hesitate to have her readmitted to hospital if she started losing weight again. Linda said she would eat provided that Sian wasn't in the room and that she was allowed to go to the bathroom after meals unaccompanied. Her parents agreed to the former but not to the latter. They also accepted that Linda was very angry with them and did not try to stop her from being rude and insulting. (The family therapist had helped assure them that this was a necessary stage of Linda's recovery.)

By this time Sian had started becoming angry with her parents and Linda, saying that they were spending far too much time bother-ing about Linda and that they were neglecting her. They didn't think this was true but the family therapist suggested that they shouldn't argue with Sian, but rather try to give her more time for herself. They agreed that the girls' mother would spend an hour each evening with Sian doing some activity that she chose, while their father would be available for Linda should she wish.

Throughout this time there had been considerable discussion

about Linda's schoolwork. It had been agreed that she shouldn't attend school while she was below a certain weight but that the school would send work home. Linda missed half a term and was becoming increasingly worried that she would not be able to catch up. Her mother, who had decided to try to work from home during this period, offered to help Linda, and they agreed to have two one-hour times during the day when her mother would be like a tutor.

Very slowly Linda started gaining weight, although some weeks were far more difficult than others. She continued to be rude to her parents and sister, and insisted on listening to her pop music at a painfully loud volume. She started experimenting with make-up and one evening dyed her hair purple without telling anyone. Her father was furious with her but her mother said she quite liked it. Linda then said that she was going to have her ears pierced and again her father was furious. Each day seemed to bring a new challenge to the parents' teamwork.

The family therapist told Linda's parents that they must reach an agreement on how to manage Linda's rebelliousness but advised that they should try to accept that she needed to express her individuality. Linda's father felt angry and confused. His previously 'perfect' daughter not only had an eating disorder but now also seemed to be turning into a 'goth'. He didn't understand what he was meant to do about it and was confused by his wife's apparent acceptance of much of Linda's behaviour. He felt his authority as a father was being undermined by Linda, his wife and the family therapist. When he said this during a family therapy session, Sian rushed to comfort him.

The therapist pointed out that this was a very confusing time. On the one hand, Linda's parents had to be very firm with regard to rules about Linda's eating, but on the other hand had to understand and accept her need to 'offload some very powerful, angry and rebellious feelings'. This led to some detailed discussions about Linda's parents' own childhood and adolescence. Both had experienced somewhat strict parenting and her father, particularly, had felt very controlled by his own father who had had very high expectations for him. Linda's father had always conformed and had not been surprised that Linda was originally such a conforming child. He felt very uncomfortable with Linda's rebellion. Her mother, in contrast, had wanted to rebel but had never dared to do so. She admitted that she obtained some vicarious pleasure from seeing Linda rebelling. A number of useful discussions were held on this theme.

Linda made a slow and somewhat fitful recovery, with some weeks proving far easier than others. By the following summer holidays, now aged fifteen, she seemed to be an altogether happier person and was showing an interest in some of the boys around. During the next school year she had to study hard for exams and shortly before they were due to begin she decided to start dieting again. By this time her parents had recognized that Linda responded to stresses such as exams, or other challenges to her self-esteem, by seeing herself as overweight and therefore ugly. On this occasion her mother had several chats with her about it and encouraged Linda to talk about her concerns rather than keeping them bottled up. Linda said that she hadn't wanted to be a bother to her parents and was sorry for all the trouble she had caused. Now that she was worried about her exams she had thought she should just put up with it and not cause more problems for her parents. Her mother gently suggested that Linda going on another diet was far more of a worry to them than her talking about her exam concerns. They were able to share a laugh about this and they agreed that they would have a chat once a week about how things were going.

Linda passed all her exams, mostly with very high grades, although getting a bare pass in one. The family therapist congratulated her on finally allowing herself to be a little bit more like a normal teenager.

Linda's story may resonate with that of your own situation. Before she became ill she was a relatively 'problem-free' child, who did well at school and did not cause her parents any anxieties and concerns, other than the usual ones. As her anorexia nervosa developed, she became increasingly concerned about her weight and eating, concealed her weight loss and angrily refused all early offers of help. Most people with anorexia nervosa are not at first able to think of themselves as ill and will be unlikely actively to seek help. Linda's story illustrates the rocky ride through the recovery process and the importance of her parents standing firm. It also illustrates the impact that the eating disorder has on all members of the family. Linda's parents worked hard at helping their daughter but suffered many moments of doubt about what they were doing. Despite feeling, when things were at their worst, that there would never be an end to the difficulties, they persevered and Linda did manage to recover.

Leanne: Bulimia nervosa

Leanne had always been a somewhat fiery girl, hot-headed, argumentative and wilful. Alex, two years older, had in contrast always been seen as the 'good' child. Leanne's father had experienced a fair amount of bullying as a child but had overcome this and had eventually become head of security at the local airport. His wife had suffered considerable ill health, including a bad back, but maintained her job as personal assistant to the sales director of an export firm.

Leanne had managed to avoid getting into any serious difficulties, despite her temperament, throughout her childhood years. However, when she was about fourteen she started mixing with a number of what her father called 'undesirables'. Leanne taunted her father by saying they were 'very desirable' and would dress in a way that made her father feel quite concerned for her safety. Despite his concerns, he took no action because her mother did not see Leanne's behaviour as anything but normal adolescence. Leanne had been experimenting with smoking, soft drugs and alcohol, and one evening she felt very unwell. The boy she had gone out with, who turned out to be much older than he had told her, offered to look after her. He took Leanne back to his place and tried to go to bed with her. Leanne became very frightened and ran out. Eventually she was picked up by a passing police patrol car and taken home. She refused to tell her parents what had happened and over the next few days became miserable and tearful. Gradually Leanne returned to her more normal self, but blamed herself for the incident. She then began to see herself as unworthy of her parents' affection and told them they should only bother about Alex, who at this time was taking exams and planning a summer job. Parental reassurance made no difference; indeed it seemed to alienate her further. Leanne noticed an increasing urge to eat and would find herself bingeing late at night after everyone else had gone to bed. Initially she did this secretively, but after a while made little effort to conceal what was happening. Because she was concerned about weight gain she would make herself sick after each binge.

Despite Leanne's parents putting locks on the fridge and food cupboard, she still managed to have regular binges. Both parents noted that money had gone missing from their wallets and that the dustbin was full of empty food packets. Eventually they sought professional help and Leanne started seeing a counsellor. Intermittently the counsellor would also talk to her parents. Leanne had apparently started blaming herself for everything that had been going wrong, including the traumatic evening out, her mother's ill health and some problems that her father was experiencing at work.

Life became more difficult for Leanne: she could not stop herself bingeing and vomiting, her schoolwork suffered and she became increasingly depressed. One evening she felt so desperate that she scratched her wrists with a meat knife and was surprised to discover that she felt a relief of tension. She did not tell anyone about this but continued to do it once or twice a week. Eventually her mother noticed the marks on her wrist and called the counsellor for advice. It was agreed that the whole family should meet with the counsellor to decide what to do. This led to a very emotional meeting in which each family member expressed their despair at what was happening. They agreed to have a series of family meetings and Leanne started a course of antidepressants.

A number of issues emerged during the family meetings: first, Alex expressed considerable anger towards her father, although it was not clear why this was; second, the father shared with his family, for the first time, details of how he was bullied as a child, and most particularly how he blamed himself for it, as if he had deserved it; finally, both parents acknowledged that there were considerable difficulties in their own relationship, which they could see had impinged upon Alex and Leanne.

The counsellor helped make some connections between all these points and recommended that the parents should have some separate marital counselling. Alex in turn asked for some counselling for herself and this was arranged. Progress was very slow and on a number of occasions consideration was given to Leanne being admitted to hospital. Gradually, however, she started gaining more control of the situation. With her parents' help she was able to recognize the triggers for binges and to devise strategies for distracting herself when the compulsion arose.

During the next year, Leanne's binges decreased in frequency, eventually occurring about once every ten days instead of nearly every day. Her other impulsive behaviour also gradually reduced as the months went by. Alex benefited considerably from counselling, although having gone through a stage of considerable antagonism to both parents and to Leanne. The parents in turn had a trial separation but eventually decided to stay together.

Leanne's story illustrates how her bulimia nervosa developed out of a combination of factors related to her personality and family situation. Her behaviour became quite chaotic and dangerous and she suffered from very low moods with self-harming tendencies. Treatment was complex, involving all members of the family, and attention was paid not only to helping Leanne gain more control over her eating habits and vomiting but also to lifting her mood and to addressing some of the factors that had contributed to the development and maintenance of the bulimia. Each member of the family had to work on their own issues, as well as working together as a family.

David: Selective eating

David had proved very difficult to wean and his mother struggled to get him off the breast. Eventually she managed to encourage him to eat a small range of tinned baby foods but nothing else. By the time he was two years old he would eat only cream-cheese sandwiches and drink milk. The doctor said he would grow out of it but he didn't. He was seen by a paediatrician who did some tests for allergies; these were inconclusive.

During his pre-school years, David's mother would sit with him for hours encouraging him to try new foods, offering rewards, but to no avail. One doctor suggested he should be forced to eat but this made things worse. When he started school David was still stuck, but was surprisingly healthy and full of energy. His parents decided that as he was not suffering physically they would not try to change his diet any more.

At the age of ten, David had a chance to travel with his school to Ireland, but expressed concern that the school staff would make him eat other foods. His parents met the teachers and asked them to let him eat whatever he could manage and not coerce him. The school asked for a medical report and then agreed to take him. He returned from the trip happy that he had managed, but concerned about some teasing.

David transferred to senior school at the age of eleven with some trepidation. Advice was sought from a dietitian but this made no difference and he refused to return to her.

For a while he seemed to cope, but as more opportunities arose to stay away from home overnight he became increasingly concerned about his problem. At the age of fourteen he asked again for help. At this point he was eating the cream-cheese sandwiches and French fries. Occasionally he would eat a pizza, but only a mozzarella-and-tomato one, and only the central bits. Despite his diet he was taller than his father and had entered puberty. He told the psychologist to whom he was referred, 'I am worried that very few girls would want to share a chip sandwich with me!'

The psychologist told David that she was willing to help but that he would have to do most of the work and that it was likely to take many months. He was so keen to overcome the problem that he agreed to do anything she said. She asked him to draw up a list of new foods he was willing to try over the next few weeks, even if only in minute quantities or just tastes.

At the next meeting he produced a list, as follows: bacon-flavoured crisps, ham pizza, white-bread sandwiches with sugar, banana, custard. The psychologist asked him to choose which he would start with and then asked him to bring the first choice to the next meeting. He chose banana.

Before attempting the banana they chatted about a number of unrelated topics, including David's favourite music. The psychologist suggested that David might bring some of the music for them to listen to next time. Towards the end of the meeting she encouraged David to try one thin slice of the banana. With enormous difficulty he approached the slice and managed to swallow it. The same process was repeated at the next meeting, after David had been advised to keep practising with a small slice each day, but this time accompanied by the sound of his favourite pop group. At the third meeting David tried some cold custard!

This extremely slow process was maintained over several months, but by the end of a year of treatment David was eating about twenty different foods. In the next six months, without any further treatment, he increased his range very considerably. He was discharged from the clinic, but wrote to the psychologist a few weeks later:

Dear Ann, just to let you know that I had a date last night. We had pizza and chips and apple pie, but I could have had lots of other things. She would never have guessed what I used to be like. Many thanks for all your help. Lots of love, David.

David is typical of many selective eaters in only eating a very limited range of foods for many years. He was able to overcome his eating difficulties largely because he wanted to, the time was right and he had a strong motivation to expand his diet. The therapist's task was relatively simple. She needed only to guide him, and to help him take things at a manageable pace to avoid frustration and disappointment.

Dominic: Restrictive eating

Dominic was born prematurely and weighed only 1.5 kg at delivery. He was kept in a special-care incubator for four weeks and seemed very weak and sickly for several weeks thereafter. He was discharged home six weeks after delivery on an enriched diet, in which he showed little interest.

Dominic's parents remained very concerned about his failure to enjoy feeds throughout his early childhood. None the less he seemed to develop normally, but was very thin. He experienced the usual childhood illnesses but never became debilitated by them. When he was four, his parents decided to take a more determined approach to getting him to eat fully. This led to enormous battles at the meal table with pleading, shouting, threatening and punishments, but no improvement in his intake. Indeed, Dominic told his parents he wouldn't eat anything after one particularly stormy session and he was true to his word for the next day. They rushed him to the doctor, who wisely told them to 'back off' as he was perfectly healthy otherwise.

Dominic's parents hoped that his appetite would improve when he started school, but to no avail. By this time he was showing considerable distress at mealtimes and seemed to dread them, as did his parents. They asked for referral to a specialist, who made the same comment as the family doctor. Dominic was growing satisfactorily and was in good health, so did not require any treatment. The specialist told them that if they continued to pressurize Dominic to eat more than his appetite allowed, it was more likely that unnecessary problems would arise. She explained that if he were not growing well then her advice might be different, and that they should just let him eat what he wanted for the next six months, after which they could review the situation.

Dominic continued to eat poorly but to grow satisfactorily throughout his childhood. He had a growth spurt as he entered puberty aged fourteen, and by the age of sixteen was 180 cm (six foot), but very thin. His many friends called him beanpole and he in turn happily called them shrimps. Dominic continued to thrive throughout his adolescence.

Dominic's story illustrates the difficulties many parents of restrictive eaters have in containing their anxieties. This is very understandable, as every parent wants to ensure that their child is eating well enough to sustain growth. Unfortunately, what often happens is that parents focus on how little is eaten and ignore the fact that the child is growing and developing normally. Some people, like Dominic, are always going to be slim, and it really does not help to be constantly pushed to eat more. The clinician's role in Dominic's case, having ascertained that he was healthy, was to do little more than reassure, and try to allay the parents' anxieties.

Sammy: Food phobia

Sammy was referred to us aged ten with a three-year history of difficulty with eating. Previously he had been a happy but slightly sensitive child, who had always been in good health. He was the only child in a very loving family, both parents fully employed and all four grandparents living nearby. He was a keen footballer, played for a school team, and one of his grandfathers would take him to watch professional games. He had many friends and did well at school.

One day he had witnessed his grandfather choke on some food, turn blue and lose consciousness. His grandfather developed pneumonia and died a few days later. Thereafter Sammy found it difficult to eat. He could manage only fluids and soft foods. He refused to eat any solid foods and was particularly frightened of lumpy foods and food with skin on it, such as fruit. No amount of persuasion or promises made any difference. He was seen by a number of doctors, none of whom could find anything wrong, despite many tests. On one occasion he was admitted to hospital for observation but this added no further information to what was already known.

Three years after the onset of the problem we saw him in our clinic. We were quite surprised to note that he was only just a bit below average height for his age but well below average weight. His parents had helped him to maintain some nutrition by providing predominantly blended foods (they had bought a food processor especially) and nutritious drinks such as milk and hot chocolate.

It was clear that Sammy suffered from food phobia having been traumatized by his grandfather's death. Although he had overcome his grief, he had remained fearful that the same thing might happen to him. Foods with skin and lumpy foods particularly frightened him because he had become hypersensitive to the texture. The sensation of swallowing anything solid made him gag and he would then become very distressed.

Although the term 'food phobia' is used to describe this problem, it is more a phobia of swallowing or choking. In any event, as is so often the case with phobias, the more the feared situation or activity is avoided, the more frightening that situation or activity becomes. This certainly applied to Sammy, who had not attempted any solid foods for over eighteen months and was absolutely terrified that we were going to try to make him eat. On the other hand, he wanted to overcome the problem because he was being teased at school.

The therapist who saw Sammy spent some time attempting to reassure him that he had no intention of trying to get Sammy to eat anything he felt unable to try. He told Sammy that he wanted to help him to work at his own pace. First, the therapist taught Sammy how to get into a state of deep relaxation, which counteracted the intense anxiety he felt. In addition, he took advantage of Sammy's enthusiasm for football by inventing a fantasy football league with him and putting the names of all the teams on a large poster. The participants in this league were Sammy and twenty foods he couldn't tolerate. Sammy was currently at the bottom of the league, since each food had got the better of him. The food immediately above Sammy was the first one he would try, the one above that the second, and so on. Each week Sammy would try to eat a small portion of the food immediately above him and if he succeeded he would move above it in the league. The aim was for him to get to the top of the league within twenty-six weeks. Sammy's parents were appointed as referees to determine whether or not he had won each 'match'. Sammy thoroughly enjoyed the idea and entered into it with enthusiasm.

At the start of the 'season' the league table looked like this:

Apples Athletic
Strawberries United

Baked Beans Wanderers
Roast Potatoes Rangers
Toast with Jam Hotspurs
Inter-Chips
Chocolate Biscuits
Fried Fish Albion
Bacon Borough
Boiled Eggs
Pizza Palace
Meat Balls
Cornflakes Real
Porridge Rovers
Weetabix Wednesday
Orange Cake Orient
Chocolate Cake Celtic
Scrambled Eggs
Spaghetti City
Rice Pudding Rangers
Super Sammy

He found the first match of the season against Rice Pudding Rangers very difficult and actually lost. It was agreed to recruit a new player to his team, a medicine called alprazolam, which he took just before the kick-off. This added strength to the team by reducing anxiety.

The next week he decided to play Spaghetti City instead of having a rematch against Rice Pudding Rangers and, according to the referees, won with ease. This meant he was now twentieth in the league with Spaghetti City below him but his arch rivals Rice Pudding Rangers still above him. He decided to try Scrambled Eggs next as he was still not confident enough for an outing against the Rangers. To everyone's delight he was successful and in victorious mood devoured both Cake teams, and went on to take great mouthfuls out of Weetabix Wednesday. He had a slip-up in the match against Porridge Rovers but, as he said, the opposition was rather lumpy.

He won his next three matches with ease, decided on rematches with those that had previously defeated him and, riding on his success in these games, he decided to play two matches a week instead of one. There were no further slip-ups and at the end of the tournament Super Sammy was the league champion.

Sammy had no further trouble with eating and for some while

after his treatment had finished he would send press cuttings to his therapist about the achievements of his favourite real football team, the one he used to watch with his grandfather.

In Sammy's case, his fear of choking had led to an inability to eat normally. It was clearly related to an event – his grandfather choking and subsequently dying – which had triggered a paralysing anxiety. His treatment was a combination of medication to reduce his anxiety and a carefully graded approach to the introduction of feared foods. His parents played an important role in supporting him through the whole process.

Paul: Food avoidance emotional disorder

Paul's parents had separated acrimoniously when he was seven years old, after some years of disharmony. He had two younger brothers, aged five and four. Paul had always been a rather fussy eater but had grown satisfactorily and had not been a cause for concern. Very soon after the separation he became miserable and 'went off his food'. His mother sought help from the family doctor, who suggested that this was an understandable reaction to his parents' separation and that, provided Paul was given plenty of reassurance (this was not defined) and time alone with each of his parents, all the problems would settle down.

Paul did seem to respond partially to more 'cuddle time' with his mother but he remained miserable and tearful, particularly at bedtime, and ate very little, to the point where his mother became alarmed by his weight loss. Physical examination and investigations revealed no physical cause and it was evident that his loss of appetite was a symptom of his underlying misery. Paul did manage to go to school and kept a 'brave face' when with friends and in front of his brothers, for whom he felt some responsibility. Undoubtedly the most difficult thing for him was eating 'I just don't feel hungry'. He had no anxieties about his weight or shape and he expressed worry about his loss of muscle.

Eventually Paul was referred to our clinic where we made a diagnosis of food avoidance emotional disorder. In other words, he was certainly avoiding food in the context of feeling miserable, but he had neither the features of anorexia nervosa or other eating disorders, nor of depression. In the latter case, he would have shown a more profound and intense lowering of mood, and generalized features of distress such as sleep disturbance, inability to concentrate at school or loss of enjoyment of TV or friendships. It is likely that eating, rather than anything else, was affected because this had previously been a slightly problematic area for him.

What we did discover from our assessment was that Paul was distressed not only by his parents' separation but also by their continuing arguments, both in front of and about him and his brothers. Furthermore, we ascertained that his parents had different ways of responding to his poor eating, with his mother cajoling and pleading with him and his father getting angry and punishing him.

Under these circumstances it was not at all surprising that Paul was having trouble eating. We agreed to meet with Paul's parents on a few occasions to try to help them resolve some of their conflicts without involving the children and to find a unified and consistent way of dealing with his eating. We emphasized the importance of working well together as parents, despite the fact that their marriage was over. They had to find a way of doing this for many years to come if the children were to be OK. This would involve considerable compromise on both their parts and there might be times when they really didn't feel they could do it.

They managed to agree that they would adopt an approach to Paul's his eating that was neither cajoling nor punitive. One of them would sit with him, acknowledge that eating was difficult and reassure him that he would not be punished for not eating and that they would do whatever they could to help. They were also advised to try to ensure that the atmosphere at mealtimes was as light as possible.

Meanwhile, we arranged for Paul to have some individual counselling. During this he became able to tell his counsellor that he felt it was his fault that his parents had separated 'If only I had been good they wouldn't have had to argue about me.' The counsellor not only explained to him that this was a common feeling for children whose parents had separated, but also arranged for Paul and his parents to be seen together. At this meeting the counsellor helped the parents jointly to explain to Paul that their separation was nothing to do with his behaviour but was simply due to the fact that they had stopped being friends and couldn't stop arguing. Understandably, this was a difficult task for his parents but the counsellor explained how important it was for Paul to experience them taking joint responsibility.

Paul gradually recovered his appetite and slowly regained his lost weight. His recovery was not smooth and it was noted that whenever he was aware of his parents arguing eating became problematic for some days thereafter.

Paul's story shows how underlying emotional difficulties can affect eating in a way that is very different from anorexia nervosa. Paul did not particularly want to lose weight; he just did not feel like eating. His distress was centred around the breakdown of his parents' marriage, a situation which is often difficult for children to adjust to. In particular, Paul as the oldest of three children would have been likely to feel a certain weight of responsibility. This is not unusual but does often require some careful discussion and working through. The counsellor in this case chose to work with both of Paul's parents, even though they were no longer living together. This is important, because to Paul they are, and will remain, his parents, even though the relationship between the two of them may have broken down.

Denise: Compulsive overeating

Denise, like her parents, had always had a very good appetite. Her mother had often found that when Denise was a baby the only way to calm her down when she was upset was by feeding her. This had become a pattern, which took hold during her early childhood. She would frequently eat large amounts and throughout her childhood was teased for being overweight.

Denise was put on a large number of different diets over these early years. None worked because she was unable to adhere to any of them for more than a day or two. She would take food from the fridge and the food cupboard whenever no one was watching, and at school had been known to take other children's food. When she was eleven she went through a spell of refusing to attend school as she couldn't tolerate the teasing.

Denise found it hard to make friends, and even those friendships she did make seemed not to last. She became a loner who took comfort from further eating and subsequently became even more overweight. Denise was twice referred to a psychologist but to no avail, and hypnosis also made no difference.

She left school aged sixteen and was unable to find work. Eventually she registered at a local college to receive further education. There she joined a local music society and discovered that she was quite a good singer who was in demand for certain parts. Gradually she made friends and gained confidence in herself. She remained a compulsive overeater and considerably overweight, but was much happier.

Denise received little in the way of treatment other than some suggestions for diets. Treatment of compulsive overeating in childhood is often difficult, and is of limited success. A useful focus is often self-esteem issues, particularly when a child is being teased for being overweight or feels so self-conscious that this is inhibiting social interaction and development. In Denise's case, self-confidence grew slowly through recognition of her abilities and achievements, gaining friends, and through being valued and valuing herself.

Postscript

If you have read this book from cover to cover, you will have heard the stories of many different children and their families. Some of the struggles, worries and difficulties you have read about may have struck a chord. Some of the situations we have described will not have been similar in their detail to your own, but even in these cases we hope that some of the ideas and comments we offer may be relevant to you.

If you picked up the book with many questions and concerns, we hope that the experience of reading it has been informative and reassuring. Reassuring not in the sense that you do not need to worry or do anything about your child's eating problem, but in the sense that there are positive things you can do to help. We have used many different examples to try to illustrate the points we have tried to make but we will not have covered every last possible concern or question. A book can never give all the answers but we hope that we have provided you with ideas and suggestions that you can now put into practice. These ideas and suggestions are not plucked from the sky; they are borrowed from other parents who have been in a similar situation to the one you may be in now but who have played an important role in successfully helping their children put their problems behind them.

Above all else, remember that you as a parent are the best person to help your child. You may at times need more help and support than at other times. It is fine to seek out that help and use it. Seeking help should not be seen as an admission of failure but as a positive acknowledgement of a difficulty that requires some additional input to help you manage it. If you are currently facing a situation that you are struggling to cope with, remember that your child too is struggling with something that she is unable to manage. Even though you may feel that you have lost sight of the child you once knew, that you are pushed away and your attempts to help unwanted, it is possible to get through this and to emerge together at the end of what may in some cases be quite a lengthy haul. Our hope is that by sharing some of the experiences of other parents with whom we have worked, we will have been able to help you some way along the road to your child's health and happiness.

Glossary

Alprazolam Tranquillizer of specific value in food phobia.

Amenorrhoea Failure to have periods, usually due to low weight.

Amitriptyline Antidepressant.

Anaemia Deficiency of blood or haemoglobin.

Antidepressants Medicines or tablets designed to relieve depression.

Asperger's syndrome Mild variant of autism.

Asthma Disorder of the respiratory tract, marked by coughing and difficulty in breathing.

Autism Disorder of childhood development, characterized by difficulties in language and social interaction.

Binge/Bingeing Eating a large amount of food while experiencing a feeling of loss of control.

Body mass index (BMI) Ratio of relative body weight derived from the formula 'weight in kilograms divided by height in metres, squared'.

Carbohydrate Substance such as sugar or starch composed of carbon, hydrogen and oxygen.

Clomipramine Similar to amitriptyline but also helpful for obsessive compulsive symptoms.

Cognitive behavioural therapy Form of psychotherapy which focuses on problem solving. Abbreviated to CBT.

Cyst Collection of fluid.

Diabetes Endocrine (see below) disorder in which a lack of insulin leads to high blood-sugar levels, treated by insulin injections and special diet.

Diazepam Tranquillizer.

Dietitian Specialist in nutrition.

Diuretic Medicine that increases the flow of urine.

Endocrine glands Organs that secrete hormones.

Fads/Faddiness Extreme fussiness.

Family therapist Clinician specializing in working with families.

Fluoxetine One of the newer types of antidepressants known as selective serotonin re-uptake inhibitors (SSRIs), useful in treating depression and bulimia nervosa.

Fluvoxamine See fluoxetine.

Follicles Cells within the ovary, which once mature produce the ovum or egg.

Forced feeding This term is generally used to mean feeding someone against their stated wishes and when there is active resistance to being fed. This is an extremely rare event (see p. 119 for discussion) and should only occur in the most extreme of situations. The term 'forced feeding' is also sometimes mistakenly used to refer to nasogastric feeding (see below), but the two should not be confused.

Gagging Sensation that combines feelings of choking and vomiting.

Genes Hereditary factors that are transmitted by parents to their children and which determine a wide range of characteristics.

Growth spurt Time during early adolescence when the rate of growth accelerates considerably.

Hypnosis State of being hypnotized, i.e. an abnormal mental state, resembling sleep, that is induced by suggestion.

Imipramine Anti-depressant.

Incubator Cabinet in which heat is automatically regulated, often used for newborn babies who are unwell.

Lanugo hair Fine downy hair commonly found on the backs of newborn babies, which reappears in the presence of considerable weight loss.

Laxative Substance that loosens or relaxes the bowel and thus encourages bowel opening.

Malignant disease Particularly serious illness in which cells are destroyed.

Metabolism The chemical changes occurring within the body.

Motivational enhancement therapy A treatment designed to increase motivation to recover, of considerable value in anorexia nervosa and over-eating. Abbreviated to MET.

Nasogastric feeding Feeding via a narrow tube, which is passed up the nose and then down into the stomach via the oesophagus. Used for feeding when the child is unwilling or unable to take food by mouth. This is not to be confused with forced feeding (see above), as children will usually agree to being fed nasogastrically.

Neuro-imaging Techniques for investigating the brain and central nervous system.

Oesophagus That part of the gastrointestinal tract that conveys food from the mouth to the stomach.

Osteopenia Thin bones.

Osteoporosis Disorder of the bones in which there is very much reduced bone density.

Ovaries Female reproductive organs that produce the ova (eggs).

Paediatrician Doctor specializing in the health of children.

Parotid Large salivary gland in the cheek.

Pneumonia Lung infection.

Polycystic ovaries Cysts on the ovaries, a complication of anorexia and bulimia nervosa, leading to menstrual irregularities.

Pre-pubertal State preceding the onset of puberty.

Prozac See fluoxetine.

Psychiatrist Doctor specializing in mental health.

Psychologist Clinician or researcher specializing in the mind and its activities.

Psychotherapy The treatment of problems using various methods of discussion rather than medication.

Purge/Purging To induce vomiting or abuse laxatives.

Relaxation technique Form of treatment that induces relaxation.

Satiety State of feeling full.

Sedatives Medicine or tablets that induce a state of sleepiness.

Serotonin re-uptake inhibitors New range of antidepressants. Abbreviated to SSRI.

Sertraline See fluoxetine. In some countries sertraline may be used only for adults.

Tranquillizers Medicine or tablets that induce a state of calmness.

Tube feeding Nasogastric tube feeding. This is not forced feeding but involves the passing of a very narrow tube into the stomach via the nose. The person is then fed via the tube with specially prepared liquid feed high in calories and nutrients.

Ulcer Superficial sore discharging infected material.

Ultrasound Technique for investigating internal organs using sound waves.

Uterus Womb.

Weight for height ratio Index similar to body mass index but more applicable to children and adolescents.

White cells (leucocytes) Blood cells that combat infection and allergy.

Further reading

Cooper, P. J., *Bulimia Nervosa: A Guide to Recovery*, London: Robinson Publishing, 1993.

Costin, C., *Your Dieting Daughter. Is She Dying for Attention?*, New York: Brunner Mazel, 1997.

Crisp, A., *Anorexia Nervosa: Let Me Be*, London: Lawrence Erlbaum Associates, 1989.

Fairburn, C., *Overcoming Binge Eating*, New York: The Guilford Press, 1995.

Hirshmann, J. and L. Zaphiropoulos, *Preventing Childhood Eating Problems*, Carlsbad, CA: Gurze Books, 1993.

Hornbacher, M., *Wasted (a survivor's story)*, London: Harper-Collins, 1998.

Lask, B. and R. Bryant-Waugh, *Anorexia Nervosa and Related Eating Disorders in Childhood and Adolescence*, 2nd edition, Hove, UK: Psychology Press, 2000.

Leese, H. J., *The Eating Habit*, Lancaster, UK: Quay Publishing, 1994.

Orbach, S., *Hunger Strike*, London: Penguin Books, 1993.

Palmer, B., *Helping People with Eating Disorders: A Clinical Guide to Assessment and Treatment*, Chichester, UK: Wiley, 2000.

Purgold, J., *The Lingering Malady: Anorexia and Bulimia*, Edinburgh: J.P. Publishing, 1991.

Schmidt, U. and J. Treasure, *Getting Better Bit(e) by Bit(e): A Survival Kit for Sufferers of Bulimia Nervosa and Binge Eating Disorders*, London: Lawrence Erlbaum Associates, 1993.

Siegel, M., J. Brisman and M. Weinshel, *Surviving an Eating Disorder: Strategies for Family and Friends*, New York: Harper Perennial, 1988.

Southall, A. and Schwartz, A. (Eds.), *Feeding problems in children: A practical guide*, Abingdon, Oxon: Radcliffe Medical Press, 2000.

Treasure, J., *Anorexia Nervosa: A Survival Guide for Families, Friends and Sufferers*, Hove, UK: Psychology Press, 1997.

Zerbe, K., *The Body Betrayed: A Deeper Understanding of Women, Eating Disorders, and Treatment*, Carlsbad, CA: Gurze Books, 1995.

Useful addresses

Australia

The Eating Disorders Association Inc.
53 Railway Terrace
Milton
Queensland 4064
Tel: 07-3876-2500
Fax: 07-3511-6959
E-mail: edu.inc@uq.net.au
Website: www.uq.net.au/eda

Anorexia and Bulimia Nervosa Association of South Australia
1st Floor
Woodwards House
47 Waymouth Street
Adelaide 5000
Tel: 08-8212-1644
Fax: 08-8212-7991

Eating Disorders Association of Western Australia
PO Box 8015
Perth Business Centre
WA 6849
Tel: 08-9487-1939
Fax: 08-9371-6853

Canada

NEDIC – The National Eating Disorder Information Centre
CW 1-211
200 Elizabeth Street
Toronto
Ontario
M5G 2C4
Freephone: 1-866-63342-20
Tel: 416-340-4156
Fax: 416-340-4736
E-mail: nedic@uhn.on.ca
Website: www.nedic.ca

ANAD – Awareness and Networking around Disordered Eating
3385 West 4th Avenue
Vancouver
British Columbia
V6R 1N6
Tel: 604-739-2070/ 1-877-288-0877
Fax: 604-730-2843
E-mail: anad01@telus.net
Website: www.anad.bc.ca

The Eating Disorder Research Centre of British Columbia
Children's and Women's Health Centre
Room E200
4500 Oak Street
Vancouver
British Columbia
V6H 3N1
Tel: 604-875-2084
Fax: 604-875-3668
E-mail: edrcbc@direct.ca
Website: disorderedeating.ca

ANAB Quebec
114 Donegani Boulevard
Pointe Claire
Quebec
H9R 2W3
Tel: 514-630-0907
Fax: 514-630-1225
E-mail: info@anebque.qc.ca

Denmark

Sylfiderne
c/o Elsebeth Sos Hansen
Max Mullers Gade 11,3.
DK-8000 Aarhus C
Tel: 45-4060-5954
E-mail: sylfiderne@city.dk
Website: http://users.cybercity.dk/~bbt1485/

Italy

ICED-Italian Centre for Eating Disorders
Via Ugo Ojetti 16
Flat 4
Rome 00137
Tel: 6-8689-6825

Mexico

Eating Disorders Mexico
Paseo de las Palmas
751–1002
DF 11010
Tel: 525-540-0493
E-mail: clinica@eatingdisorders.com.mx
Website: www.eatingdisorders.com.mx

New Zealand

Christchurch Eating Disorders Service
The Princess Margaret Hospital
Cashmere Road
Christchurch
Tel: 03-337-7707
Fax: 03-337-7789
E-mail: eds@cdhb.govt.nz

Eating Difficulties Education Network (EDEN)
4 Warnock Street
PO Box 78 005
Grey Lynn
Auckland
Tel: 09-378-9039
Fax: 09-378-9393
E-mail: info@eden.org.nz

Eating Disorder Services
PO Box 13 807
Johnsonville
Wellington
Tel: 04-478-6674
Fax: 04-477-4160
E-mail: info@eatingdisorders.org.nz
Website: www.eatingdisorders.org.nz

Norway

Anorexia/Bulimia Foreningen (ABF)
Postboks 36
5001 Bergen
Oslo
Tel: 47-5532-6260
Fax: 47-5532-5701
Website: www.lilleapo.no/hjelp/sporsvar.html

Regionalaudeling for Spiseforstyrrelser
Divisjonsledelsen i psykiatri
Ullevål Universitetssykehus
0407 Oslo
Tel: 47-2211-8462
E-mail: Perjohan.isdahl@ullevaal.no

South Africa

Anorexia and Bulimia Support Group of South Africa
PO Box 84295
Greenside 2034
Johannesburg
Tel: 027-116-462-809/027-082-777-0528
E-mail: ronhey@iafrica.com

Spain

ADANER – Associación en defensa de la attención de la anorexia
nervosa
Calle Mirabel 17, 5 D
28044 Madrid
Tel: 1-91-5044347

Switzerland

ABA – Association Boulimie–Anorexie
Avenue de Villamont 19
1005 Lausanne
Tel: 021-329-0439
Fax: 021-329-0409
E-mail: info@boulimie-anorexie.ch
Website: www.boulimie-anorexie.ch

UK

Eating Disorder Association
1st Floor
Wensum House
103 Prince of Wales Road
Norwich
Norfolk
NR1 1DW
Youthline: 0845 634 7650
Helpline: 0845 634 1414
Fax: 01603 664915
E-mail: info@edauk.com
Website: www.edauk.com

St George's Child and Adolescent
Eating Disorder Service
Harewood House
Springfield University Hospital
61 Glenburnie Road
Tooting
London SW17 7DJ
Tel: 020 8682 6747

Great Ormond St Feeding and Eating Disorders Service
Department of Child and Adolescent Mental Health
Great Ormond Street Hospital
London WC1N 3JH
Tel: 020 7829 8679
Fax: 020 7829 8657
Website: www.gosh.nhs.uk

USA

The National Eating Disorders Association
603 Stewart Street
Suite 803
Seattle
WA 98101
Tel: 206-382-3587
E-mail: info@nationaleatingdisorders.org
Website: www.nationaleatingdisorders.org

Academy for Eating Disorders (AED)
6728 Old McLean Village Drive
McLean
VA 22101
Tel: 703-556-9222
Fax: 703-556-8729
E-mail: aed@degnon.org
Website: www.aedweb.org

ANRED – Anorexia Nervosa and Related Eating Disorders, Inc.
P.O. Box 5102
Eugene
OR 97405
Tel: 541-344-1144
E-mail: jarinor@rio.com
Website: www.anred.com